SKATING ON THIN ICE

A ZEN PATH OF SELF-REALIZATION

EZRA BAYDA

KONSTELLATION PRESS

Published by Konstellation Press, San Diego

www.konstellationpress.com

ISBN: 979-8-9868432-1-6

Copyeditor: Lisa Wolff

Cover design: Scarlet Willette

To all those who may fall through the cracks in the ice but not know how to become free.

CONTENTS

PART III

FOREWORD

"All truly worthwhile thoughts are conceived by walking." Nietzsche

I've been walking—meaning living—for almost eighty years. In writing this book, my intention has been to only write about what I know from my own experience—the thoughts reached by walking. I see myself as a practical philosopher, in that the teachings are primarily on how to live.

The philosophy presented in this book is the summation of my fifty-five-year-long spiritual journey. Some of the material had its genesis in my prior writings, but all of it reflects my own evolving experience.

I am happy to share what I've learned with others, but my primary intent in writing this book is more personal. It is meant to be a reminder and an inspiration for whatever remains of my own path of self-realization. I have found that it's very easy to forget what I've learned—both big things and little things. I'm at the point in my life where I don't want to forget. I want to rekindle the quiet but joyful wisdom that I've been fortunate to experience, and provide inspiration to carry on, especially as the light begins to fade.

PART I

1

THE HUMAN CONDITION

The basic underlying condition that all of us share—that we are all vulnerable and at the mercy of uncertainty—is a reality we'd rather not think about. This basic human condition is aptly portrayed in a picture I have on my wall of a girl ice skating. She's gliding along with her arms held high and her head thrown back. She seems carefree, but only because she's ignoring the sign that says "Beware of Thin Ice."

Don't most of us glide through life on automatic pilot? Maybe our life is going well—we may have supportive relationships, good physical health, and perhaps a decent job. Yet even as we glide along, there's a part of us that knows how thin the ice beneath us really is. We can sense the anxious quiver inside of us, rooted in a sense of vulnerability. We may sense a vague dissatisfaction, pain that is not yet healed, and fears that have not yet been addressed. Still, most of the time we choose not to look.

When our life takes a turn for the worse, when we start encountering cracks in the ice, we may make our usual efforts to push away or overcome the difficulties. Or we might try to skate around the cracks by ignoring or suppressing our reactions to unpleasant events.

In an attempt to keep from falling through the cracks in the ice, we choose our strategy, either working harder at maintaining the illusion of control or trying to escape from our difficulties with diversions, pleasures, or busyness. Rarely do we question our strategies—and as a consequence our life narrows down to a sense of vague dissatisfaction.

Sometimes we have to fall right into the icy water, unable to move or breathe, overwhelmed and drowning, before we're forced to deal with the deep-seated conditioning that runs our life—all the landmines of anger, fear, and confusion. It might take an illness, a financial upheaval, a relationship failure, or the death of someone close to us to wake us up and force us to deal with the icy water.

How we work with these most difficult situations will be a measure of how we understand what our life is truly about. The degree to which we can welcome our difficulties, say Yes to them—*Yes, I'm willing to experience this in this moment*—is not only a measure of our courage, but also the key factor in our ability to open to and appreciate our life.

THE THEME of skating on thin ice has been an influential force in my worldview since my mid-twenties, when I remember reading about someone shooting at people from the rooftops in New York City. Events like this are much more common in current times, but for me it was a first, and the randomness of the killings struck me deeply.

This theme of the unpredictability of life was strongly reinforced in the early seventies, when my former wife and I bought a house with a little land in Northern California. For eleven years we cultivated an extensive organic garden. Our goal was to live from the land, which included raising goats for milk and chickens and sheep for meat, as well as canning and freezing organic fruits and vegetables for year-round consumption. It was a nice life, and we felt satisfaction in being able to raise our children in the healthiest way we knew how.

But when my wife and I both came down with severe immune system disorders, high levels of DDT residue were found in our blood. The DDT had been buried on our property prior to our owning it, and the poisons had made their way into our bodies indirectly through the vegetables and meat that we were so carefully raising. The prolonged exposure consequently broke down our immune systems. Ironically, the effort to live a healthy organic lifestyle contributed to the onset of chronic debilitating disease.

There was no one to blame. Burying the leftovers was just what people did to dispose of pesticides in those days. As a consequence, our strategy to make our world safe and secure had failed. We had been, unknowingly, skating on thin ice.

No matter what we do, no matter how good our intentions are, there's no way we can guarantee that we can avoid having difficulties—sometimes falling right into the icy water.

The real issue is whether or not we will learn when our strategies fail.

When my life fell apart with the onset of the immune system disease, it took me quite a while to really understand the great teaching embedded in honestly facing our most difficult circumstances. Even something that is obviously unfair can be our teacher.

PART of this teaching is understanding that our difficulties are not obstacles on the path of self-realization—*they are the path itself.*

BEFORE WALKING the path of self-realization, we take everything as either a blessing or a curse, whereas after entering the path we learn to take everything as an opportunity. They are opportunities to awaken and become inwardly free.

Can we learn what it means to be open to an unwanted situation, with its sense of groundlessness, as a wake-up call? Can we look at it as a signal that there is something here to be learned?

When hardship strikes, it is essential to learn not to point the finger of blame—at another person, at ourselves, at an institution, or even at life itself—and instead to turn our attention inward. When we're in distress, this is often one of the hardest things to do, because we so want to defend ourselves. We so want to be right.

What is much more helpful is to look at what we ourselves have brought to the situation—beliefs, expectations, requirements, and cravings. Then we might gradually come to the understanding that whenever we're having an emotional reaction, it's a signal that we have some self-limiting belief system within ourselves that we haven't yet looked at deeply enough. With practice, this understanding gradually becomes our basic orientation.

For example, when my wife and I first got sick from

the hidden pesticides, I got very afraid and very angry. It would have been easy and seemingly justified to rail against the unfairness of the situation. But I also had the choice to look inward.

When I saw that my anger was based in my deeply seated expectation that life was supposed to be fair, and that my fear was based in the realization that I had little control in the situation, it was possible to step outside of my anger and fear and more easily deal with the situation for what it was.

What we need is a gradual yet fundamental change in our orientation to life—toward a willingness to just be with whatever we meet. Perhaps there is nothing more basic and essential than this willingness to just be.

To simply be with our experience—even when feeling heavy and dark—can engender a sense of lightness and heart. The willingness to learn from our disappointments and disillusionments is key.

Perhaps pain we thought we could never endure becomes approachable. As we cultivate our willingness to just be, we may even discover that almost everything is workable.

Until we come to know what this means, we are cutting ourselves off from the openness, the connectedness, and the appreciation that are our human potential.

2

SELF-OBSERVATION

Developing the "observer" is key. The observer's focus is objective—it is not analytical. It is the part of our mind that simply sees what we do, how we think, what we think about, how and when we react, what our basic persona strategies are, what our core fears are.

In observing ourselves objectively in all kinds of situations, we can begin to see clearly much that we were not previously aware of: specifically, our fear-based ideas about how we're supposed to be, how others are supposed to be, how life is supposed to be.

CONSIDERING that we can deceive ourselves about anything, honest self-observation is often a study in lying and living from illusions.

SELF-OBSERVATION IS NOT about wandering through the mazes of our mind, as in introspection. Instead, the subject of self-observation starts with our physical body. For example, we can observe our posture, gestures, movements, facial expressions, and especially the physical sensations in the body that accompany our emotional reactions.

Self-observation is also not about free association or memories that may be triggered. It is always about what is observed in the present moment.

And the attitude is nonjudgmental. Any "should" is antithetical to genuine awareness.

The more honest we are at looking at ourselves, at seeing through our blind spots and control strategies, the lighter we become. Why? Because in becoming more aware, we can give up our unnecessary baggage—the self-images that we cling to, the pretenses, the someone special to be.

THE FIRST TIME I met a famous Zen teacher was in a formal interview at a retreat, and I was anxious about how to relate to this teacher. I sat down and told her my name, and she asked me, "Where are you from?" I immediately froze in fear; I thought she was asking me the ultimate Zen question. When I answered, "I don't know," she burst out laughing, and said she meant where did I live!

I had come in with so many assumptions—about what Zen was, what a famous Zen teacher would be like, who I was supposed to be—and it never occurred to me to inspect these pictures I was living from. I had bought into my pictures as uninspected truths.

. . .

We sometimes wonder how people can't see the most obvious things about themselves—yet we forget those people are us!

By a strange quirk of the human mind, each of us seems to think we are special, that we are the center of the universe. To protect ourselves we build walls—not just external walls like on our borders, but also walls in our minds—walls of identity, of religion, race, and gender.

Once they are in place, by another strange quirk of the human mind, we actually believe that these illusory walls are real, and we use them to perpetuate our protective stance of Me versus Them.

Yet, part of the path of self-realization is to see through these illusory walls. Just because another person may be different from us doesn't mean they are a threat. Perhaps we can even enjoy and appreciate the differences, which can engender the experience of the connectedness that we are.

Our greatest insanity, and also deepest self-deception, is believing our illusions as the unquestioned truth.

Self-observation is greatly enhanced by what is called "beginner's mind." Beginner's mind is a term in Zen Buddhism that describes a mind that is eager, without preconceptions, and open to possibility. As Zen teacher Suzuki Roshi once said, "In the beginner's mind there are many possibilities. In the expert's mind, there are few."

One way to invoke beginner's mind is to go back to the fundamentals of meditation practice, which are rooted in two essential questions: "What's going on right now?" and "What is my practice in this situation?" You could spend a long time working on nothing but these two questions, and it would no doubt be very fruitful.

Let's start with the first question: "What's going on right now?" At the most basic level, what's going on at the moment is that you're reading this book. But what else is going on? I find it helpful to break that down into three components: the physical, mental, and emotional.

Starting with what's going on physically, there are three specific areas you can always bring your attention to. The first is your posture. Feel it now and adjust as necessary. The second is your facial expression. We're rarely aware of the subtleties of our facial expressions. Feel it now, particularly the tension around the mouth and eyes, and soften any tension. The third is overall bodily tension. Feel the whole of yourself, almost as if you were outside of yourself, and then soften and relax into the body.

Next, what's going on right now mentally? For example, is the mind clear or foggy? Perhaps it's sleepy or dull. Perhaps it's agitated. The point is just to be aware of what's happening in our mind, not judging that any mental state is particularly good or bad.

Here it's often helpful to ask another question: "What am I adding?" For example, we may notice our worries, or our judgments, or one of our endless stories about how we think things are. We may notice our own particular patterns of thinking that we add to the present moment and tend to get caught in, such as planning, conversing, or fantasizing.

After checking in with the physical and mental components of what's going on, check in with your emotional state. Are you contented, emotionally neutral, or discontented? Again, it's helpful to notice what we're adding to the present moment. For example, what tone or mood are you adding? Are you bored? Anxious? Angry? Notice any subjective filters.

The point of asking what's going on right now and doing precise physical, mental, and emotional check-ins is to take the first step to wake up from our sleep.

Interestingly, there's always more than one thing going on. But if we're honest, most of the time we're hardly aware at all. And if we *are* aware, we're usually only aware of one aspect of our being, such as physical discomfort or emotional distress.

"What's going on right now?" is the fundamental first question in all of our practice; it's the first step out of waking sleep. The suggestion is to ask this question repeatedly throughout the day, especially when we feel we're somehow stuck.

Once we're aware of what's actually happening in the moment—what we're feeling and believing—the next crucial question is: "What is my practice in this situation?"

In answering this question, the most important thing to remember is that practice is possible in only one place: here, right now. So what we're specifically experiencing will determine what our practice will be. For example, if you're experiencing monkey mind—the mind that jumps from one thing to another, the mind that spins in thoughts—ask what would be a good practice to work with that. How about if you're sleepy or caught in emotional upset or self-judgment? What if nothing special is going on—what's the best practice in that situation?

. . .

We have to remember that at times practice can seem very confusing. Sitting in meditation, we may sometimes wonder, "What exactly *am* I doing here?" We wonder if we're supposed to be staying with our breathing, noticing thoughts, or just trying to reside in the stillness. When strong emotions or deep beliefs arise, we might be even more likely to forget what we're supposed to do. So many of us, for example, forget to do loving-kindness practice when we get caught in self-judgment.

If at any given moment you were to pause and ask yourself, "What is my practice right now?" a lot of the time the honest answer might be, "I don't know." This confusion doesn't arise because there are too many different practices to choose from—it's simply because we temporarily forget what we know. Half of what I do when talking to students is to remind them of what they already know.

If we can remember to ask the final question, "What am I leaving out?", that will often point to what we need to do. For example, we might be leaving out awareness of the breath, or the body, or the environment. We might be leaving out the labeling of our believed thoughts, or the crucial perspective of seeing our difficulties as our path. It will no doubt be helpful if, in our practice, we address whatever it is we're leaving out.

If, day by day, moment by moment, we continue our self-observation by asking ourselves the essential practice questions, we will keep beginner's mind—and a world of possibility—alive.

3

A FUNDAMENTAL PROBLEM

Once a farmer went to tell the Buddha about his problems. He told the Buddha about his troubles farming—how either droughts or monsoons made his work difficult. He told the Buddha about his wife—how even though he loved her, there were certain things about her that he wanted to change. Likewise with his children—yes, he loved them, but they weren't turning out quite the way he wanted. When he was finished, he asked how the Buddha could help him with his troubles.

The Buddha said, "I'm sorry, but I can't help you."

"What do you mean?" railed the farmer. "You're supposed to be a great teacher!"

The Buddha replied, "It's like this. We all have problems—it's a fact of life. Sure, a few problems may go away now and then, but soon enough others will arise. So, we'll always have eighty-three problems."

The farmer responded indignantly, "Then what's the good of all your teaching?"

The Buddha replied, "My teaching can't help with the

eighty-three problems, but perhaps it can help with the eighty-fourth problem."

"What's that?" asked the farmer.

"The eighty-fourth problem is that we don't want to have any problems."

ALTHOUGH WE MAY NOT KNOW it, we all have the deep-seated hope that our problems will disappear. And beneath this hope lies an even deeper one: that life should be free from pain.

Although hopes and beliefs such as these are often what brings us to a path of self-questioning and self-realization, a life free of difficulties is not what that path is about.

The path of self-realization is ultimately about becoming inwardly free. As we travel the path, it's possible that our relationship to our problems will, in fact, become less burdened. But as conditioned beings living in a messy world, we will *always* have difficulties. We will always have "eighty-three problems."

Expecting our problems to go away is truly our fundamental problem.

AN ILLUMINATING story is told by Tibetan teacher Pema Chödrön. She tells about a childhood friend who had recurring nightmares in which ferocious monsters would chase her through a house. Whenever she would close a door behind her, the monsters would open it and frighten her. Pema asked her what the monsters looked like, but her friend couldn't answer because she never really looked.

However, the next time she had the nightmare, just as

she was about to open a door to avoid being caught by the monsters, she was somehow able to stop running, turn around, and look at them. Although they were huge, with horrible features, they didn't attack; they just jumped up and down. As she looked even closer, these three-dimensional colored monsters began to shrink into two-dimensional black-and-white shapes. Then she awoke, never to have that nightmare again.

It is the pushing away of our "monsters" that makes them so solid. As we begin to see through the solidity of this resistance, our lives become more workable.

BEFORE WE ENTER the path of self-realization, we see our experiences in terms of "good" or "bad." Upon truly entering the path, we see them only as opportunities to awaken.

TO WILLINGLY INCLUDE whatever we encounter, not to push the unwanted away, is what it means to truly be with our life, to say "Yes" to it. But we can't force ourselves to say "Yes" any more than we can meaningfully say the popular phrase "No problem!" "No problem!" does have, on a profound level, a real meaning; but it falls far short as long as we hold onto our deep-seated desire not to have any problems.

That we'll try to hold onto this desire is a given—it's what humans do. Yet, on the path of self-realization, our only real option is to include all of our experiences. Pushing away the present moment of our experiences guarantees that we will suffer.

Sometimes we may have strong emotions that can even feel like death. But they are *not* death. In fact, they are nothing more than a combination of believed thoughts and strong or unpleasant physical sensations.

As we cultivate the willingness to just be with the physical experience of an emotion, this fact can gradually become clear to us. With perseverance and effort, we discover that it is possible, through staying present with the unpleasant emotion, to transform these solid emotional reactions into something much more porous. It's not that they disappear (although they might), but that we hold them much more lightly.

4

THE PRESENT MOMENT

Most forms of spiritual practice put an emphasis on being in the present moment. But why do we seem to so often want to move away from the present moment? We even do it when the present moment seems positive. Sometimes we move away, almost as if the present moment were dangerous.

ONCE I WAS SITTING in the front row at a meditation center. The head teacher was sitting in front of me, directly facing me. I closed my eyes and started following my breath, gradually feeling the presence and comfort of the spaciousness of the breath. Then, seemingly out of the blue, I started to feel intense emotional discomfort. The discomfort rapidly turned into panic, and it was all I could do to not jump up and run out of the room. Apparently, my pride—not wanting to be seen as a failure by running out—was stronger than my fear.

So I sat there, with my heart beating so loudly I

thought everyone could hear it. I was also sweating profusely. I couldn't imagine my failure as a meditator being any more obvious.

But then, out of desperation, I came back to focusing on the breath—primarily to get away from the panic and intense bodily discomfort. I made my focus more and more intense, and gradually began to include the overall experience in my body, as well as the environment of the room.

Then, the miraculous happened. It was as if I walked through a doorway into another world. My panic and fear completely disappeared, and all I could feel was an overwhelming experience of peace and love.

This experience taught me what it means to be serious. It isn't about attaining a pleasant state of mind. Nor is it about being somber. It means to take nothing as seriously as the resolve to attain inner freedom.

Yet, how often are we really present in this way? How often can we say to the present moment, "This is what I want"? Not longing for the past or looking for something new or different in the future, can we be content with exactly what our life is in that moment?

As we truly reside in the present moment, less caught up in our thoughts, there is a loosening of "me-ness." Being without the familiar ground of self-identity can indeed feel dangerous, as it did for me when I first started to feel present in the example above. The more we let loose, the stronger the sense of danger. In my example the danger moved all the way to panic.

Yet, truly staying with the present moment transforms us because it permeates the seeming solidity of our tightly knit sense of self, with all of its painful and unwanted emotions.

When we stop identifying with this narrow sense of

"self," as I did almost as an act of desperation, we can start identifying with the wider and more spacious context of what life is. This is where I tapped into the incredible experience of connectedness and love.

OUR WILLINGNESS TO be present with the physical reality of the present moment allows us to connect with Life—beyond the many layers of our psychological conditioning.

THIS APPROACH IS CERTAINLY NOT new. Stoicism, from ancient Greece, is often dumbed down to refer to having a stiff upper lip, or emotional reserve. But Stoicism is actually an ancient tool for remaining present and inwardly calm when in adversity. The Stoics understood that we can find meaning even in being alone. When many of us were isolated during the coronavirus lockdown, we felt the pain of being away from our friends, pleasures, routines, and social life. But the great Stoic Seneca taught that being truly present with a bit of deprivation can be an excellent corrective to becoming accustomed to living a soft and decadent life.

He wrote: "Until we have begun to go without them, we fail to realize how unnecessary many things are. We've been using them not because we needed them but because we had them."

Perhaps, during this period of relative isolation, you were able to experience that being present with what we might ordinarily consider hardships allowed you to get back to the essentials and renew your sense of purpose.

Perhaps, amidst the constant news of suffering and death, you became aware of the fact that we don't have endless time. There is nothing more potent than this realization to wake us up to the preciousness of living in the present moment.

THERE'S AN APHORISM THAT STATES: "Everyone has pain. Everyone suffers. Everyone will die." Taking this to heart —not in a morbid way—can spark our aspiration to not waste our life.

5

EXERCISE: THREE-BY-THREE

In learning to be truly present, many have found helpful the meditation exercise called a "Three-by-Three." It's an exercise in expanding your awareness muscle, and it's designed so that it's not that difficult to do. In this practice, you bring three different aspects of sensory input into awareness simultaneously and hold them for three complete breaths.

FOR EXAMPLE, first bring awareness to the sensations of the breath, and now, while staying with that, begin to include the sense of touch in your hands as they rest in your lap. And now, while staying with awareness of breath and touch, expand your awareness to include the perception of sound; and hold all three together for three complete breaths.

ANOTHER EXAMPLE: Again, bring awareness to the sensations of the breath. Be sure you are feeling the physical quality of the breath, not just the thought of the breath. Now, while maintaining awareness of the breath, expand awareness to include the physical feeling of your posture. Now, while maintaining awareness of the breath and your posture, add to awareness the feeling of the air on your skin. Feel the temperature and the texture of the air. Hold these three components—the breath, your posture, and the air—in awareness for three full breaths.

YOU CAN DO this for several rounds of three breaths, using a variety of focal points: your feet, the top of your head, your mouth, back, or buttocks. You can use sight (shapes, colors, shadows) or any prevailing sensations or tensions in the body. The point is to expand the awareness, based in physical reality, and hold it without slipping back into thought. In directing awareness to the three different points of focus, we experience more fully what is happening right now.

THIS EXERCISE MAY BE difficult in the beginning, but when you do it over and over the container of awareness gradually widens. At some point you may experience a literal jump into what is sometimes called the "witness" space, where you no longer identify solely with the sense of "me" that is our usual orientation. This usual orientation is the basis for our basic state of waking sleep.

MEDITATION, when practiced regularly, can open us in ways we could not have imagined. The fruit of meditation is a serene inhalation of what is most real, with an exhalation filled with gratitude and kindness.

6

DETOURS AND STRATEGIES

There are three major detours that we use to avoid the present moment. The first is analyzing. When a difficult situation arises, one of our first reactions might be to ask why. We analyze the situation by asking, "Why is this happening?"," Why am I depressed?", "Why am I so tired?", "Why am I anxious?", and so on. We ask why, in part, because we want certainty; we want to maintain the illusion that our lives are guided by certainty and logic. We want to avoid the anxious quiver of the present moment, the discomfort of not having ground under our feet.

The second major detour is blaming. In blaming, we focus on the perceived faults of the other, to detour away from having to direct our attention inward, which we fear might be extremely uncomfortable. Blaming always separates; it always disconnects. In fact, when we're caught in blaming, the sense of "me-ness" is never more solid.

The third major detour is judging, especially judging ourselves. Our deep-seated self-judgments arise early on from the inevitable disappointments of our formative years. Over time, these judgments become more and more deeply ingrained, until eventually, they become what we believe to be The Truth. Until we begin work with our self-judgments, these negative, painfully demeaning beliefs will not even be open to question.

Just as the food we eat can either nourish or pollute the body, our experiences can also either nourish or deplete our spiritual being. Whenever we engage in self-centered thoughts or actions, such as our self-judging, we are feeding the growth of our little self; conversely, our conscious life-centered actions help feed our basic Being.

"Bad" food, or experiences that we engage in without awareness, also often drain us and leave us depleted of the energy that we need to make genuine efforts to grow inwardly. Perfect examples of this are our detours of analyzing, blaming, and self-judging. Equally draining are our strategies of control, such as trying to prove ourselves or trying to please everyone.

When we play out these strategies, we are usually so caught up in them that we are living in the ultimate self-absorption, and the energy it takes to maintain them often leaves us feeling drained. At the same time, we remain full of anxiety.

HERE IS the essence of the problem: As humans, we have an innate craving for safety, security, and comfort. As a consequence, we develop our strategies of control early on to ensure that these cravings are met. But because these strategies become so dominant, our lives begin to narrow, and we are increasingly disconnected from our true nature, our naturally open heart. The energy necessary to awaken is thus squandered by trying to maintain the illusion of control.

. . .

YET, no matter how hard we try to maintain our illusions, aren't we all just one doctor's visit away from the total loss of control? I certainly felt this loss of control when I was told, out of the blue, that I had a cancerous tumor on my kidney. And I immediately went into the strategy of trying to regain control. But because these strategies often afford at least some form of temporary relief, we remain on the treadmill of our strategies until we realize, at times too late, that we're running on empty.

There are three common strategies of control: trying harder, seeking approval, and escaping/numbing.

On a subtle level, the strategy of trying harder leaves us with the underlying feeling of restlessness, unable to do the simplest, yet most valuable thing, which is to reside in the moment and feel at home there. The need to *do* something, to be active, is so strong that for many people, the simple act of sitting still, with nowhere to go and nothing to do, is the most frightening thing. The fear that arises—from the felt sense of an inner lack—can range from anxiety all the way to full-blown panic. Ironically, learning to stay with this sense of lack, with the frightening feeling of being no one special, is how we ultimately learn to see through it.

THERE IS A VERY deep satisfaction born of being able to occupy a space without an agenda—to enjoy the inner equanimity of just being, however and wherever we find ourselves.

. . .

Seeking approval is the second almost universal control strategy. Wanting approval is natural—it's the instinctual survival mode of wanting to be liked in order to fit into the herd. But at a very early age we turn it into something else, when we start using approval seeking as a control strategy to mask our insecurities, to avoid feeling the pain of our core delusions of unworthiness. The belief is: "If I can get you to like me, I won't have to feel the pain of being unworthy."

We may know in our mind that seeking approval is a dead end, and that we can only do so much to please people, but our body still carries the tension of believing that we *should* be able to please everyone all the time. Of course, all of this is based on the core fears of feeling unworthy or of not being enough.

One key in working with the control strategy of seeking approval is to become able to welcome and say Yes to the base fear of unworthiness. Saying Yes means we are willing to reside in it—to *feel* it, experiencing it on a visceral level in the body. This may not be easy or comfortable, but it's ultimately much less painful than living in a state of constant anxiety that demands external approval in order to feel okay.

The third almost universal strategy of control is escaping or numbing, when we either use diversions to escape feeling distressed or shut off and go numb.

All of us, to some extent, employ the strategy of seeking diversions, whether it be through entertainment, food, alcohol, drugs, or even staying busy. These addictive behaviors all have one thing in common: avoidance of the pervasive inner feeling of unease.

But the relief we get from pursuing this strategy is always temporary, and as we continue to follow these compulsions, we squander energy while still not finding any abiding satisfaction. In fact, our addictive behaviors, whatever they might be, often bring self-judgment and shame, which deplete our energy even further.

Numbing ourselves is the other very common strategy of control, and in its most subtle form is maintaining the belief that we have endless time. This illusion, which we all hold onto to some degree, leaves us convinced that our life will continue indefinitely into the vague future.

We are rarely aware of the extent to which this belief has us skating on thin ice, oblivious to the very real fact that our lives can end or be drastically altered at any time, without any warning or preparation. We choose to stay oblivious, to cruise through life on a numbing automatic pilot, so that we don't have to consider anything unpleasant.

Our agenda with all of these strategies is to feel comfortable, yet our capacity to understand that life itself doesn't have an agenda, particularly *our* agenda, seems to be very limited. We insist on our sense of entitlement that life gives us comfort, pleasure, and ease.

WHY CAN'T we understand that the fullest and richest experience of life is often the result of the difficulties that life presents, where we are forced to go deeper? Isn't disappointment often our greatest teacher?

ONE THING I learned from a long period of being sick: my illness, including the unending discomfort, is not all of who I am. On many occasions, as I would lie there, staying with the breath and trying to stay out of my head, with all its anxious thoughts, my awareness would shift to a much more spacious perspective, including a larger sense of myself beyond the physical body.

The point of living is not simply to maintain comfort in the physical body. When we know the point of living, we can put up with many things that otherwise might seem unbearable, including the breaking down of the body. When we are committed to the path of self-realization, when discomfort arises, instead of following our usual detours and strategies of control, we come to understand that our very discomfort is our exact path to becoming inwardly free.

Yet, because this understanding is so counter to our conditioned way of seeing the world, we may continue to believe that we have a problem whenever we feel discomfort. If we have anxiety in the chest or poor sleep, we lament our problem. But life never promised us comfort or good sleep.

Our real problem is not that we have discomfort, but that we don't have discomfort about what really matters —discovering how to truly live an authentic life.

WE SHOULD NEVER UNDERESTIMATE our desire to be comfortable; and on the path of self-realization, we need to recognize over and over again the strength of our desire to avoid both physical and emotional pain.

We also need to continually return to the essential human problem that the path of self-realization addresses—that we don't know who we are, that we feel disconnected from our true nature.

Our basic tools—seeing our thoughts clearly and physically feeling the reality of our life—are enhanced as we cultivate the mindset that's willing to welcome a difficulty—to say Yes to it. This mindset grows with the increasing unwillingness to stay complacent.

Saying Yes allows us to move toward unknown territory, even while the voice of fear tells us to stop. As we understand that without this step we will forever remain stuck, there's a willingness to enter into life in a new way.

It's good to remember that whenever we make sincere efforts, we will soon trick ourselves in order to abandon our quest. The countermeasure is to persist in spite of all the barriers and disappointments.

7

PERSEVERANCE AND CURIOSITY

Underlying all of our efforts on the path of self-realization is the quality of perseverance. Perseverance means that we are steadfast, regardless of how we feel. Even when we don't feel motivated, or can't quite remember why we're practicing, at least we know the necessity of not giving up. We know the need to at least show up.

THE PROTAGONIST in the book *The Way of the Pilgrim*, by an anonymous Russian pilgrim, is a perfect example of the meaning of perseverance. The book is the story of a simple pilgrim who walked across the plains of nineteenth-century Russia. He carried only dried bread and two books—the Bible and the Philokalia, an instruction for Eastern Orthodox monks—to sustain his body and his practice. With a genuine homesickness for God, his only aim was to learn how to pray without ceasing.

Although we're unlikely to ever be pilgrims in the old-fashioned sense, there is something real in the phrase "pray without ceasing." Real prayer is a genuine surrender to the moment, whatever the moment may be. It's not like the prayer of children in the sense that we're asking that our wishes be granted. Real prayer is a deep opening to life itself, a deep listening, a willingness to just be with the moment.

In this sense, it is essentially no different from the practice of opening into the heart. By entering into the spaciousness of the heart, we're allowing life to just *be*.

What most gets in the way of this deep form of prayer is just what the pilgrim experienced: the constant desire to spin off into the comfort and security of thinking—into our plans, fantasies, dramas, and especially our believed judgments.

How do we counteract this very human tendency? Just like the pilgrim, we bring awareness to the breath, the heart, or the words of prayer over and over.

This is not easy. The pilgrim started with thirty minutes of prayer a day. Then his teacher told him to recite the prayer two thousand times a day. Then six thousand. Then twelve thousand. After years of practice, with wholehearted devotion and perseverance, the prayer became self-activating and he could pray without ceasing. He experienced the delight of the heart bubbling over and gratitude toward all things. He came to understand the meaning of the words "The kingdom of God is within."

For the pilgrim, perseverance was the key. In fact, persevering, in the face of discouragement and resistance, is often where our learning goes deepest. There are times for all of us when resistance can be very powerful, where we may feel totally lost in our quest. Who hasn't experienced thoughts like "I'll never get this", "I'll never make the efforts that are necessary", or "What's the point?" Yet, to continue to practice—to persevere—even when we don't remember why is how we learn to go deeper into our life.

In *Thus Spoke Zarathustra*, Nietzsche wrote: "Today your courage & your hopes are still whole. But the time will come when that which seems high to you will no longer be in sight, and that which seems low will be all-too-near. And you will cry, 'All is false!' There are feelings which want to kill our aspiration; but if they do not succeed, well, then they themselves must die."

During this process, there is a point at which an essential shift occurs in our Being, where we move from a predominant orientation toward sleep and mechanicalness—whose primary goals are comfort, security, approval, and control—to a growing orientation toward wanting to live more awake.

This shift is not like a change in mood, or a temporary phase, or even a change in attitude; it is an actual change in our state of Being. This shift deepens our willingness to persevere, and although strong emotions and old patterns may resurface once in a while, fundamentally there is no turning back from the path of self-realization.

Without this shift in our Being, we will always be at the mercy of our moods, desires, opinions, and emotions, as well as of our ever-changing external circumstances. In other words, we will perpetuate our old ways of seeing and being, thereby maintaining a life of sleep and mechanicalness.

So what is it that changes? And how? First, we have to ask, who are we to begin with? For example, what is an "Ezra" other than a physical body with a personality? Yet, don't we try to protect this "Me" at all costs?

To make the change or transformation possible, we first have to see how serious we are about the little things —our upsets, our discomforts, and so on—without being serious enough about the bigger things, such as realizing our true nature.

We're uncomfortable when we feel rejected, lonely, or unappreciated, but we're not nearly uncomfortable enough about how asleep we are, or how self-centered we are. Nor do we often enough feel the discomfort of how disconnected we are from ourselves and others, and how rarely we experience the Love that is our nature.

AGAIN, perseverance is essential, but it is not enough by itself. With perseverance alone, it is tempting to become almost militant and stoic in practice. We might even become grim. So to balance this essential component, we also have to cultivate the softer quality of curiosity.

Curiosity means that we're willing to explore unknown territory—the places the ego doesn't want to go. Curiosity allows us to take a step at our edge, sometimes toward our deepest fears.

Unfortunately, our innate curiosity is often stifled at an early age. Our wanting to know, as well as our natural delight in knowing, is easily covered over by seeking approval or predictability, and therefore hard to access.

Asking the question, "What is my experience right now?" is the essence of practicing with curiosity, in that the only "answer" comes from being open to actually experiencing the truth of each moment.

EARLY IN MY PRACTICE, from studying Nietzsche, I learned the expression *Ja-sagen*, or "Saying Yes to life." But saying

Yes is not just a philosophy or an affirmation. Saying Yes is an existential response to life, especially when it is difficult. It is about a willingness to enter into and feel what our life actually is.

This involves the essential element of curiosity—simply wanting to know the truth of the moment, even when part of us is telling us to turn away. Every moment of resistance—and resistance is ongoing for all of us—is an example of saying No. No, I don't want to feel that. No, I don't want to be present with that. This is why saying Yes, with curiosity, is essential.

Being truly curious means we're willing to say Yes to even the hard parts, instead of indulging the No of our habitual resistance.

Saying Yes doesn't mean we like our experience, or that we necessarily *feel* accepting. It doesn't even mean that we override the No. Saying Yes simply means that we pay attention—meticulous attention—to the No. It means we're no longer resisting the people, things, and fears that we don't like; instead, we're learning to lean into them in order to experience what's actually going on.

For example, as we walk the path of awakening, we come to understand that having anxiety doesn't mean that something is bad. All it means is that there is anxiety, the feeling of skating on thin ice, which is simply the result of our own particular conditioning. With this understanding we are no longer so caught up in "me and my difficulty," but more able to relate to the difficulty from a larger sense of what life is.

Ultimately, practice requires the implicit understanding that whatever situation or emotion we can't say Yes to is the exact direction of our path. So if anxiety arises, we don't have to fight it. Nor do we need to fix it. In fact, instead of viewing it as a problem, we simply pause, acknowledge it, and then say "Hello" to it—which means welcoming it with curiosity as an opportunity to work with our own particular edge. Remember, we don't have to like the anxiety. We just need to *feel* it as the physical experience that it is. And then we rest in it and learn from it.

And when we rest in it and learn from it, we no longer identify with the I of "I-as-anxious," but rather with "I-as-Awareness." Within that larger sense of Being, the anxiety is not a particular problem.

Sometimes it seems that we can't say Yes to our experience. Perhaps the experience is too powerful or too overwhelming. The voice of fear says "No!"—it warns us to close and defend; but another part of us says "Yes!"—calling us to open and connect. And the way we do this is by breathing the uncomfortable sensations directly into the center of the chest on the in-breath; then on the out-breath simply breathing out—allowing us to possibly experience the healing power of the heart.

THE FUNDAMENTAL POINT is that until we become intimate with our difficulties and fears, until we can welcome them with curiosity, they will always limit our ability to love.

IN OTHER WORDS, the path to living from genuine kindness requires giving our willing attention to the very things that seem to block the way to it.

8

THE FIVE ESSENTIAL QUESTIONS

Many people come to meditation practice with the expectation that it will calm them and relieve the feelings of distress. Certainly, meditation can do this to some extent; however, when we're knee-deep in emotional distress, we're fortunate if we can remember what to do. Even if we could remember to meditate, simply sitting down to follow the breath, without directly addressing our difficulties, is unlikely to bring a deep or lasting peace of mind. The difficulties most likely remain.

Sometimes, when emotions are particularly intense, it is especially difficult to remember what we know. And there's a good reason for this. When we're distressed, the "new" or conceptual brain tends to stop working. This is called "cognitive shock," which turns off the cognitive mind's basic ability to function. When the thinking brain is on sabbatical, we simply can't think clearly.

During cognitive shock, the "old" brain, which is based on survival and defense, takes over. At this point we're likely to attack, withdraw, or go numb, none of which are conducive to awareness. To be honest, when caught in cognitive shock, we're fortunate if we can even remember that we want to be awake.

When clarity becomes obscured by the dark and swirling energy of emotional distress, it is useful to have some concise reminders to bring us back to reality. The real question is: *What helps us awaken?* The answer to this overarching question can be broken down into five very straightforward and specific smaller questions, each of which points us in the direction of clarity.

1. What is going on right now?

This simply requires honestly acknowledging the objective situation. But to do this, we have to be able to see the difference between our view of what is happening and the actual facts of the situation.

For example, when we're caught in the swirl of emotional distress, we almost always add the thought "something is wrong"—either wrong in general or, more likely, wrong with another person or with ourselves. In addition, we will almost always think about how to escape from the distress—through trying to fix the situation, or through blaming or analyzing.

In short, working effectively with our emotional difficulties requires that we first see clearly what is actually happening apart from what we're adding to the situation, through our detours, escapes, and judgments.

Asking the first practice question—*What is going on right now?* —can help us get out of the poisonous loop of our mental stories.

. . .

2. Can I see this as my path?

If we don't ask this crucial question, we're unlikely even to remember that this is our opportunity to awaken. Yet, it is essential that we understand that our distressful situation is exactly what we need to work with in order to be free.

For example, the person we find most irritating becomes a mirror—you could call this person "irritating Buddha"—reflecting back to us exactly where we're stuck. After all, the irritation is what we add.

It is absolutely fundamental that we learn that when difficult situations and feelings arise they are not obstacles to be avoided, but rather these very difficulties are, in fact, the path itself. They're our opportunity to wake up out of our little protected world; they're our opportunity to awaken into a more genuine way of living. This point can't be overemphasized.

Remembering the importance of this allows us to make the critical practice step of welcoming our distress, because we understand that as long as we continue to resist our experience, we will stay stuck.

3. What is my most believed thought?

Answering this is like taking a snapshot of the mind. This question is tempting to skip over, especially since we often take our opinions as Truth, and it can be difficult to see what we're really believing.

Even though observation of the mind allows us to see our superficial or surface thoughts with clarity, the deepest beliefs often stay below the surface. Thus, these deep-seated beliefs often dictate how we feel and act, and they continue to run almost unconsciously.

For example, our deeply believed thoughts of personal insecurity may not be evident on the surface in a given situation; truthfully, we're often unaware of their presence. But their poisonous footprint often manifests itself in our anger, blame, depression, and shame.

These deeply believed and well-hidden thoughts of insecurity thus act like radar, and we often seek out experiences that confirm that our beliefs are true—the classic self-fulfilling prophecy. For instance, if you believe that life is not safe, all you have to do is get a bill that's a little bigger than you expected, and your mind will start weaving scenarios of doom.

We have to know where we get stuck in our particular radar-like beliefs. And we have to know how to work with them. Again, the process begins with asking yourself, *What is my most believed thought?* However, if the answer doesn't come, you drop it, and return to your physical experience, rather than trying to figure it out with the mind. Then, a little while later, you ask the question again. Sooner or later, with perseverance, the answer will present itself.

It's at this point that we begin to remove some of our investment in our deeply seated negative beliefs about ourselves. But to get to this place, first we must inquire into what our most believed thoughts are.

4. What is this?

This question, perhaps the most important one, is actually a Zen koan, in that it can't be answered by the thinking mind. The only answer comes from entering directly into the immediate, physical experience of the present moment.

Right now, ask yourself, "What is this?" Even if you don't feel any distress, this question can apply to whatever the present moment holds. Become aware of your physical posture. Feel the overall quality of physical sensations in the body. Feel the tension in the face, chest, and stomach.

Include awareness of the environment—the temperature, the quality of light, the surrounding sounds. Feel the body breathing in and out as you take in this felt sense of the moment. Feel the energy in the body as you focus on the "whatness" (rather than the "whyness") of your experience. Only by doing this will you answer the question *What is this?*

Admittedly, it is difficult to maintain awareness in the present moment when distress is present, because to truly experience the present as it is means we have to refrain from our most habitual defenses, such as justifying, trying to get control, going numb, seeking diversions, and so on. The sole purpose of these strategies is to protect us from feeling the pain we don't want to feel. But until we can refrain from these defenses, and feel the physical experience directly, we will stay stuck in the story line of "me," unaware of what life really is in the moment.

For example, if we feel anxiety, it's natural to want to avoid feeling it. We may get busy to occupy ourselves, or try harder, or try to figure it out. But if we can ask ourselves *What is this?* the only important and real answer comes from the actual physical experience of anxiety in the present moment.

Remember, we're not asking what it's about, which is analyzing—the opposite of being physically present. We're simply asking what it actually is.

It's important to understand that being able to ask *What is this?*—and truly reside with what we find there—takes a great deal of patience and courage. Maybe we can only do it a little. But we persevere—even if it's just three breaths at a time.

Ultimately, it's awareness that heals. It's awareness that allows us to reconnect with the heart, the heart that is the essence of our being.

Some time ago I was told I had to have a medical procedure to determine whether or not I had prostate cancer. Combined with the fear around the thought of having prostate cancer were the memories of painful experiences of prior similar medical procedures, leading to a feeling of dread and morbidity.

Over the years I've become free of many of my fears and attachments, but each of us has our own particular edge—that place beyond which fear tells us not to go—so even though I had extensive experience practicing with illness and pain, there was no doubt that this particular set of circumstances put me at my personal edge.

It was helpful to answer the first question—*What is going on right now?*—because I could see that there was actually no physical discomfort other than the discomfort triggered by believing in my fear-based thoughts.

It was also helpful to ask myself, "Can I see this situation as my path?"—pointing to the opportunity to work with my own particular attachments and fears.

As well, asking *What are my most believed thoughts?* allowed me to see that thoughts like "This is too much" and "I can't do this" were just thoughts—thoughts that were not the truth, no matter how true they felt in the moment.

But the real key to working with the panic and dread came from answering the koan–question *What is this?* The answer was to come back again and again to the physical experience of the present moment, such as the sensations of tightness in the chest and queasiness in the stomach. Sometimes I could only stay with it for the duration of three breaths.

Sometimes the experience was so strong that all I could do was breathe the sensations into the center of the chest, while remembering all those others who were suffering from the same or similar distress, and wishing compassion for all of us.

Staying with the *What is this?* question eventually allowed the self-imposed prison wall of fear to begin to dissolve, and I was able to experience the grace and freedom of surrender.

When we can viscerally enter into the question *What is this?* we will see that our experience, however unpleasant, is constantly changing, and that at bottom, it is just a combination of believed thoughts, physical sensations, and old memories. Once we see this, the experience of distress begins to unravel into its individual aggregates, rather than seeming so solid. Again, it's awareness that heals.

5. Can I let this experience just be?

This is not easy to do, because our human compulsion toward comfort drives us to want to fix or get rid of our unpleasant experiences. To allow our experience to just be usually becomes possible only after we've become disappointed by the futility of trying to fix ourselves (and others). We have to realize that trying to change or let go of the feelings we don't want to feel simply doesn't work.

Allowing our experience to just be requires a critical understanding: that it's more painful to try to push away our own pain than it is to feel it. This understanding is not intellectual, but something that eventually takes root in the core of our being.

Once we can really let our experience be as it is, awareness becomes a more spacious container, within which distress begins to dismantle on its own.

Sometimes it helps to widen the container of awareness by intentionally including the awareness of air and sounds, or whatever we can connect with outside the skin boundary. Within this wider and more spacious container, the distress may even transform from something heavy and somber into pure, nondescript energy, which is more porous and lighter. The energy may then release on its own, without any need to try to get rid of it.

This final question—*Can I let this experience just be?*—also allows the quality of mercy or loving kindness to come forth, because we're no longer judging ourselves or our experience as defective. We're finally willing to experience our life within the spaciousness of the heart, rather than through the self-limiting judgments of the mind.

These five questions—What is going on right now? Can I see this as my path? What is my most believed thought? What is this? Can I let this experience just be? —remind us of the key steps needed to work with our emotional distress. Some students carry little laminated cards with the five questions in their pockets for times when "cognitive shock" takes hold, when everything we know is temporarily forgotten.

Remember, though, these questions are just pointers;

it's important not to get lost in the technique. In the bigger picture, we ask these questions because when we have emotional distress, we are usually caught in our own self-imposed prison walls—of anger, fear, and confusion. But when our self-imposed prison walls come down, what remains? The answer: just Being.

9

HAPPINESS

The understanding that all is well doesn't come from making happiness the goal—it comes from being able to appreciate the journey, particularly the present-moment experience of our life. To "enjoy the ride" doesn't mean we're going to get somewhere, or get something, or become someone else; it means we're curious about what our life is and able to appreciate it—even the most difficult, unpleasant, unwanted aspects of it.

In this sense, we can say that true happiness is more about being present, being awake, being open, than it is about being happy in the Hollywood sense of being merry and cheerful.

It may be difficult to understand how it is possible to experience happiness in light of the undeniable and ongoing suffering in the world. For example, when we open our hearts and minds to what is actually going on, how do we respond to the fact that we're not taking care of the planet or providing for the twenty-four thousand people who die every single day from hunger—many of them being children under the age of five?

How do we reconcile facts like these with living a happy life, with being able to appreciate the beauty of the mockingbird singing with abandon or the majesty and wonder of the ocean? This is the crux of the human dilemma—abiding in the paradox that includes both the bleakness and the wonder. Although it may at times be very difficult to find this balance, it is, in fact, possible.

HERE IS one thing we need to remember: instead of trying to stamp out behaviors we don't like, the path to true happiness requires our openhearted attention to the very things that seem to block our way to it—especially to all the things we are most inclined to run from, reject, change, or be rid of.

Thus, when we're unhappy, rather than making happiness our goal, we must try instead to see that *whatever* is on our plate is our opportunity to work with and free ourselves from what gets in the way of happiness.

ONE OF THE most powerful barriers to being truly happy is being caught in divisive emotional reactions, such as anger, fear, and despair. Yet these very reactions can serve as an accelerated path to transformation, from the narrow self-centered world of Me to the equanimity of true contentment.

Sooner or later in spiritual practice we will have to address the inevitable clash between what we want and what is—the clash out of which all of our separating emotional reactions, and much of our unhappiness, arises.

Over the years, as we observe our emotional highs and lows, we will come to one inescapable conclusion: the way we view ourselves—as a solid, permanent self—is one of our most deeply seated illusions.

A more realistic view is that we are a complex collection of many "Me's." In one moment, we may believe strongly that life is too hard and that we can't cope. Then, ten minutes later, we can feel that everything is fine. Or, we wake up feeling anxious or grouchy, and this Me totally colors our perception of reality. But sooner or later that Me will be replaced by another Me that may seem equally real and true. Once we understand that our emotional life is strongly determined by whichever Me is presenting itself, we can learn to take a step back.

ONE INTERESTING PRACTICE is called "It does." Whenever I catch myself believing in one of my many Me's, such as when I hear myself thinking or saying, "I'm irritated" or "I'm feeling crummy," I change the words to "*It's* irritated" or "*It's* crummy." This simple change in language immediately makes the perspective more spacious, and I no longer feel so invested in that particular Me as the truth. Understanding that we are composed of many Me's, and labeling each Me as "It," fosters a sense of lightheartedness and a taste of emotional freedom.

ONE OF THE other major blocks in the way of happiness is our deeply rooted sense of entitlement. In fact, this is a big part of the "problem" of happiness: we firmly believe that we *should* be happy. We think it's our right, and consequently, we feel entitled to it.

This expectation can have many faces. For example,

we often feel entitled to good health, expecting that we can and should be able to stay youthful and physically fit. When life comes along to greet us with illness or injury, we can easily sink into a stupor of frustration and even despair. Sometimes just getting a cold will trigger our anxieties over losing control and feeling powerless.

This sense of entitlement—which basically says that life should go the way we want and expect it to go—even tells us we shouldn't have to experience discomfort. Then, when we do experience discomfort, we feel that something is wrong; we might get angry and feel it's unfair, or we may feel sorry for ourselves.

One way to become aware of our specific beliefs and fantasies whenever we're feeling low is to ask ourselves the following question: "*How do I think it's supposed to be?*" This question will usually point us directly to our specific expectation or entitlement.

Perhaps the most basic belief underlying all of our feelings of entitlement, our "if onlies," and even our illusions, is the belief that life should please us, that life should be comfortable. All of our resistance to life is rooted in our wanting life to be pleasing, comfortable, and safe.

When life gives us something other than what we want—the job that isn't satisfying, the relationship that isn't quite working, the body that ages or breaks down—we resist. Our resistance can manifest as anger, or fear, or self-pity, or depression; but whatever form it takes, it blocks our ability to experience true contentment.

WE SEE our discomfort as the problem, yet it's the belief that we can't be happy if we're uncomfortable that is much more of a problem than the discomfort itself. One of the most freeing discoveries of an awareness practice is when we realize firsthand that we can, in fact, experience equanimity even in the midst of discomfort.

A WHILE BACK MY WIFE, Elizabeth, and I went to Paris, and on our first day there I started feeling pretty flu-ish, with a bad sore throat. When we went out for a walk, it started raining, and by the time we sat down to rest in Notre Dame Cathedral, I was feeling pretty crummy, and it had all the makings of A Miserable Moment.

So, I asked myself: what's blocking happiness right now? And the answer was obvious. It was the story of the future—about how I wouldn't be able to enjoy our time in Paris if I was sick, about how it might rain for four days, and so forth.

But by dropping the story of the future, just staying with the actual physical experience of the present moment, the potentially miserable moment became an experience of just mildly unpleasant physical sensations.

Yet more than that, I realized that the present moment included sitting next to Elizabeth in one of the most beautiful churches in the world. As I surrendered to the experience—sore throat and all—the experience became one of a deep and quiet joy, despite not feeling well.

IN FACT, what blocks genuine happiness the most is being caught in the thinking mind—lamenting about the past or worrying about the future. For instance, worrying about the future, left unchecked, can turn into full-blown catastrophizing, where everything seems dark and unworkable. In addition, it can seem *real*, and cause us unnecessary distress over a situation that isn't even happening and that may, in fact, never happen.

The Stoic Seneca wrote: "We are more often frightened than hurt, and we suffer more in imagination than we do in reality."

It may be helpful to keep a notebook where you write down *your most believed thoughts.* It's very likely you will find the same ones recurring regularly, even in very different situations. For example, in depression, it is common to keep repeating versions of three of the classic thoughts associated with feeling depressed: "My world is grim," "My life is hopeless," and "I'm no good."

With almost every disconnecting emotion we entertain thoughts like, "Something is wrong here!" or "I have to fix this." And, depending on our own particular history, we get caught believing "I'm not good enough," "Life isn't safe," "I'll always be alone," or some other version of what we're conditioned to believe.

IT'S important to note that genuine happiness is not the same as the absence of unhappiness. We can be gliding along through life with our good health, a decent job, and satisfactory relationships but still not even come close to experiencing the depth of equanimity and appreciation that is possible for us.

When we're caught up in the complacency of our routines, living our life on autopilot, even if we're somewhat buffered from being actively unhappy, this is still the classic case of skating on thin ice. We're oblivious to what is really going on; all it takes is one crack in the ice—a serious threat to our health, a lost job, a relationship failure, or even something as small as being criticized or cut off on the freeway—to show us how fragile our personal "happiness" really is. We can then see how our normal happiness is just a false sense of stability, based on favorable, yet temporary, external circumstances.

THE BASIC QUESTION we need to ask ourselves is: Why do we continue to follow behaviors that don't bring us real happiness? The answer lies in the basic human condition: that is, we are born with the innate craving for safety, security, and control—this is an integral part of our survival mechanism. We are also born with an aversion to discomfort and a natural desire for comfort and pleasure. Given these basic human predispositions, it makes sense that our learned strategies of behavior are geared to ensure that our cravings and desires are met.

Yet, grasping after happiness doesn't bring happiness; it only perpetuates the grasping mind.

WHEN WE BRING awareness to our many layers of conditioning, and to the struggles that arise out of our conditioning, the power of that conditioning is slowly diminished. This is how we can begin to experience and live not so much from the Me but more from our natural Being.

As we increasingly connect with a vaster sense of what life is, we may even have moments where we're acutely aware that we *are* the vastness, as well as a unique manifestation of it. This is where the words *connectedness* and *love* become more than just words, and it is where genuine happiness comes forth naturally.

Being truly present allows us to appreciate the sweetness of the moment even when the moment isn't conventionally sweet, because, at least momentarily, we're not under the sway of the heaviness of our beliefs. The results are a lightness of being and a sense of inner freedom.

Awareness renders a definite sense of presence, of aliveness. Sometimes the experience is one of vivid wakefulness, of "I Am Here." This is not the little "I" of the ego; it is the larger sense of who we are.

Being present essentially means we're no longer caught in the head, in all of our self-centered thoughts, judgments, and expectations. We no longer identify with our thoughts or our feelings as who we are, but rather we identify with a vaster sense of what life is.

10

GRATITUDE AS A ROOT OF HAPPINESS

One of my favorite quotes attributed to the Buddha is "Let us rise up and be thankful, for if we didn't learn a lot today, at least we learned a little, and if we didn't learn a little, at least we didn't get sick, and even if we got sick, at least we didn't die; so, let us all be thankful."

GRATITUDE IS one of the essential aspects of being truly happy, because if we're not grateful for what we have, we will always want life to be different from what it is—a demand that will surely guarantee our unhappiness.

There's a Tibetan slogan that says, "Be grateful to everyone." What is this asking of us? Because it clearly sounds unrealistic, if not impossible. Are we supposed to be grateful for our roommate who doesn't clean the sink, or our boss who doesn't appreciate us? Are we supposed to be grateful for someone who criticizes us?

Of course we are! Because from the point of view of spiritual practice, *whoever*, or *whatever*, pushes us to our edge—to that place where we're stuck, and beyond which we don't want to go—is our teacher, and takes us to the exact place where the deepest learning takes place.

Take the example of the roommate who doesn't clean the sink. Why should we be grateful? Because the roommate is pointing us to exactly where we're stuck—in our anger, in our self-righteousness, in our judgments about how things should be.

How about the person who criticizes us? Why should we be grateful? Because the situation gives us the opportunity to address the hurt and fear that we would probably otherwise ignore—the very hurt and fear that prevent us from experiencing genuine happiness.

One technique to help us both deepen our learning and feel gratitude for our life is called Nightly Reflection. Right before going to sleep, I review my day, asking the question, "What am I most grateful for?"

And then, as I review my day, starting with when I first woke up in the morning, my mind can pinpoint those experiences during the day for which I feel appreciation, even though I might not have acknowledged it at the time. And with each thing I pinpoint, I silently say to myself, "I'm grateful for that."

By doing the nightly reflection regularly, I not only become more grateful during the meditation itself, but I also become more aware and receptive during the day. For example, I begin to notice that as I go through my daily routine, little positive moments are often not even acknowledged. But as I become more attuned to what is actually happening during the day, these moments begin to stand out, and gratitude is more likely to arise in the present moment.

. . .

Practicing mindfulness, or awareness in everyday life, can also foster gratitude. For example, when I'm aware, I begin to notice even the simplest thing, such as how turning on a faucet brings us water. So instead of taking running water for granted, which most of us do, we cultivate awareness and appreciation. After all, having running water is certainly not our birthright; the majority of people throughout history, and many millions even today, do not have this luxury.

Awareness allows us to appreciate such things and also to recognize our sense of entitlement, but it is only through intentional practice, such as the practice of reviewing our day each evening and reflecting on what we're most thankful for, that we actively cultivate the awareness that's necessary to make gratitude a major root of our happiness.

"If the only prayer you said in your whole life was, 'thank you,' that would suffice."

—Meister Eckhart

11

GENEROSITY AS A ROOT OF HAPPINESS

Many years ago, I heard a proverb that went something like this:

If you want to be happy for an hour, eat a good meal;

If you want to be happy for a day, make love;

If you want to be happy for a year, get married;

If you want to be happy for a lifetime, live an honest life.

I didn't find the last line quite satisfying, so for several weeks I reflected on it, questioned it, wrestled with it, until one day the answer I was looking for came to me: "If you want to be happy for a lifetime, give yourself to others."

LIVING MAINLY to get something for ourselves is a prime source of our unhappiness. The alternative is to give from the generosity of the heart. When we truly offer ourselves to someone in need—whether they are hungry or sick or deprived in some way—we experience the gratitude of living from the awakened heart, and we feel the fulfillment of acting from a sense of our basic connectedness.

A line from Ernest Hemingway's *A Farewell to Arms* has stayed with me for many years: "When you love you wish to do things for." Our deepest happiness comes when we live from this place, attending not only to ourselves but to the welfare of others.

Yet paradoxically, even though we know we are happier when we do things for others, research shows that when we're given the choice between doing something self-serving and doing something altruistic, more often than not we will choose the self-centered alternative. Sadly, as this research shows, we don't always do what makes us happy.

When we see others in need, there may be an instinctive desire to help, but the natural generosity of the heart can be overridden in a microsecond by the mind. The fear-based thinking mind raises doubts: "I don't know what to do" or "I can't get involved."

The heart that wants to reach out can easily be closed down by fear or self-protection. For example, we may fear failure or rejection. Or we may be blocked in our desire to give by our own laziness—not wanting to leave the comfort of the familiar.

Perhaps most often we get caught in our negative self-judgments, believing that we're not enough. These judgments limit us and hold us back, even when we feel the sincere desire to give. Even the belief "I'm not a giving person" may be enough to prevent our innate generosity from coming forth.

Our inherent wish to give can also be undermined by

unconscious agendas, such as wanting to get something in return. For example, many people volunteer at places like hospice or veteran's groups because they want to assuage feelings of guilt, or increase their feelings of self-esteem. Even though giving to get may feel good superficially and can motivate us initially, it is never genuinely satisfying, and we miss the natural happiness that results from giving without self-centered agendas.

THE REAL KEY to being happy for a lifetime is to give oneself to others, like a white bird in the snow. When we're truly generous, we blend in with what's going on. This means giving to others without ulterior motives or a sense of self-importance. We're not drawing attention to ourselves, and our giving isn't just another way of propping up our self-image.

Giving ourselves to others, like a white bird in the snow, means we're able to drop our agendas, including being motivated by the idea that we *should* be more giving.

Sometimes we will discover that giving doesn't seem to produce tangible results. For example, when we genuinely extend ourselves to others who are feeling alone and isolated in their pain, we may be able to do very little to take away their suffering. But in some cases, it's enough to just let another person know that someone cares, and at the very least they know that they are not alone.

My favorite quote from Gandhi is relevant: "It's the action, not the fruit of the action, that's important. Even if our action doesn't bear any fruit, that doesn't mean you stop doing the right thing."

When we drop our pretenses and the need to be a

"helper" or someone special, we can simply be present with someone in their suffering. A bond arises, and the other person may know, even if it's not conscious, that we're there with them—with an unspoken connection of the heart.

Then there are those times when there's nothing we can give or do that makes even this small relief possible. It can be very painful to see that even our best efforts sometimes don't seem to bring any positive change. We may end up judging ourselves mercilessly for not being caring enough or worthy enough. We may see ourselves as weak, or ineffective, or lacking in compassion. We may feel discouragement or even anger that the person "rejected" our kindness, our help.

In these moments, it is helpful to breathe our own painful experience directly into the center of the chest, and extend loving kindness not only to the other in their pain but also to ourselves in our discouragement, in our anger, in our frustration.

This compassion toward the whole situation allows us to continue; and eventually we can tap into the profound sense of connection and gratitude that comes when we can once again offer the generosity of the heart, regardless of our attachment to the outcome.

This deeper, more genuine experience of happiness is the natural state of our Being when we are not so caught up in our self-centered thoughts and emotions.

This is the experience of true contentment, of being fundamentally okay with our life as it is, no longer so attached to getting what the small mind of ego wants, nor demanding that life be a particular way.

. . .

The purpose of human life is not to be happy, although we certainly all want that; the purpose of human life is to awaken to who we truly are. The more we are in touch with who we really are, the closer we are to living from genuine happiness.

As we learn to reside in our experience of the present moment, we gradually discover that our true nature of connectedness is without bounds. The only reason we create the limited world of beliefs and conditioned behaviors is to make sense of things and survive.

Yet when we remain solely in this bounded world, we are cut off from the mystery of our Being, as well as from the true contentment of living from the openheartedness that is our true nature.

From this place of connectedness, our deepest aspiration is to give from the natural generosity of the heart.

Although there is no "secret" to living a genuinely happy life, the deepest happiness of equanimity grows with our ability to stay with present-moment reality, which flowers as we water the roots of the generosity of the heart—including our inherent capacity for gratitude, loving kindness, and forgiveness.

As we see what blocks genuine happiness, we discover what we have to give up so that our natural happiness can come forth. When we give up the busyness of the thinking mind and reside in the physical reality of the present moment, we can experience the equanimity of being at home with ourselves.

When we give up our entitlement, we can experience a genuine appreciation and gratitude for life.

When we give up our judgments, especially our self-judgments, we can experience the openhearted friendliness of loving kindness.

And when we give up our sense of a separate self, and tap into the reality of our basic connectedness, we can live from the natural generosity of the heart.

12

TEN GUIDELINES TO TRUE CONTENTMENT

Everyone wants to be happy, but rarely do simple formulas for happiness really help. To be genuinely happy—not just with the superficial happiness that comes when things are going well—we must learn how to be fundamentally okay with our life just as it is. This is not so easy, but here are ten specific guidelines that definitely can help.

1. **Examine your entitlements.** Take some time to reflect on what you feel entitled to, including feeling entitled to happiness. Having entitlements guarantees ongoing disappointment, yet, when we see them clearly, they lose their power.
2. **Get out of your head.** We probably spend at least 95 percent of our time lost in our head—in thoughts, worries, plans, and fantasies. Getting out of your head and coming back to physical reality—like the simple awareness of

the breath—cuts through the power of your thoughts that dictate how you feel and act.

3. **Refrain from judging yourself.** This is crucial, since much of our unhappiness comes from believing that we're not enough. To the extent that we can recognize our self-judgments, and then refrain from indulging them, we increase our ability to experience true contentment.
4. **Curb your addictive behaviors.** Everyone has some behavior that they're addicted to: exercise, the internet, overeating, people pleasing, trying harder, and on and on. The goal is not to destroy our addictions, but to understand that these behaviors only provide temporary satisfaction. When we see this clearly, we're already somewhat free of them.
5. **Learn to pause.** This is especially important when we're caught in an emotional reaction, such as anger. Pause, return to awareness of the texture of your breath, and simply try to feel the breath for the duration of three breaths. This allows you to step out of the mental melodrama, and perhaps have a refreshing taste of reality.
6. **Meditate daily.** Meditating every day, even if only for twenty to thirty minutes, helps us learn to be at home with ourselves as we are, which is essential for experiencing genuine equanimity.
7. **Practice gratitude.** Every night before going to sleep, remember what happened during the day that you are grateful for. Often, we forget

to be appreciative, yet being grateful is one of the essential attributes of being truly happy.

8. **Learn to give in relationships.** Think of one thing you can give that the other person wants, such as truly listening to them, or not criticizing them. As you give, you learn that happiness is more about giving than about getting what you want.
9. **Learn to give at work.** Instead of thinking about work in terms of what you'll get, think about what you have to offer—your own unique gifts, including doing an undesirable task as well as possible. Giving from the natural generosity of the heart is a key to true contentment.
10. **Practice forgiveness.** If there is anyone you can't forgive, invite them into your heart. Instead of seeing the person as your enemy, try to understand that whatever they did came from their own pain. To experience forgiveness is like letting go of a heavy burden. Forgiveness is freedom. Forgiveness is genuine happiness.

REMEMBER that we don't have endless time. Without this remembrance we will sleepwalk through life, not being aware that our lives can end or radically change at any instant. When greeting another, silently say to yourself, "Everyone has pain. Everyone suffers. Everyone will die." This will help cultivate a compassionate heart.

13

ATTACHMENT

One of the biggest detours on the path of self-realization is our attachments. We're all a slave to our attachments, and we make the choice every day to cling to them.

But at some point, we have to make the choice between happiness and attachment. Do we want to be attached or do we want to be happy?

The answer is very clear—we want to be attached! For example, even though we can see that our desires give us ephemeral pleasure at best, why is it that we still cling to them? Because we won't give up the *belief* that they will in fact eventually make us happy.

Will money or position make us happy in the sense of a deep or residing satisfaction? It doesn't take much to see that they won't. Yet, we still pursue them, because we still *believe* that they could. The point is: attachment is very difficult to see clearly within ourselves.

. . .

Much of my insight into the power of attachment came out of struggling with the intense identification I've had with my daughters. The most prolonged and fruitful struggle centered on my younger daughter Jenessa's basketball career.

We had played basketball together since she was ten years old, and by the time she reached high school, she was the star of her team. When she played well, I would feel great, and when she had the occasional off game, I would feel horrible. Though I tried to work with these ups and down, since she usually played well, I was less motivated to explore my attachment, because it usually felt good.

When Jenessa went to college, she had a great first year. But in the very first game of her sophomore year, she tore a knee ligament, which sidelined her for the remainder of the season. Although we were both disappointed, we could still look forward to the following year.

But that next season turned out to be very difficult. As hard as she worked, the year off had taken its toll, and her body wasn't quite in sync with the game. The physical difficulties led to limiting beliefs that became mental difficulties. As I watched Jenessa struggle, in my gut I experienced the power of attachment.

Of course, as a father I naturally felt bad for my daughter. But that wasn't the problem. The problem was my identification with her success. I was living from the belief—the illusion—that my happiness depended on how well she played. My attachment to this belief was so strong that during and after the "bad" games, I would feel the sensations of dread and doom in my stomach.

From the perspective of practice, it was good news that the disappointment was so strong, because it really got my attention. I felt the extent and the power of my attachment and how it imprisoned me.

So I started viewing Jenessa's games as an opportunity to study and work with it. When her game was off and I'd experience a sinking feeling and the mild nausea of anxiety, I'd check to see what beliefs gave rise to my emotional/physical reactions.

Soon I began to see what was going on: I was attached to *my* accomplishments. Because I was so identified with Jenessa—seeing her as an extension of myself—I was experiencing her accomplishments and her "failures" as my own.

As my attachment became clearer and its power diminished, I found that I could enjoy my daughter's efforts even when she didn't excel. During the last two years she played, I was grateful for being increasingly able to appreciate *her*, apart from my own neediness and attachment.

Attachment is always a barrier to real appreciation and happiness, because it's based on the illusion that some external element can make our core pains go away. But when we're willing to expose ourselves to the pain we've been avoiding, the power of attachment fades and the path to a genuine life becomes more accessible.

When we *see through* our attachments—which means fully seeing and experiencing them—the result is inner freedom.

AGAIN, the simplicity and clarity of practice amounts to this: first, we must see through the mental process, dropping the story line of "me." What is the story line of "me"? It's the attachment to comfort, to our thoughts, to our self-judgments and emotions, to our identities and our fears.

WHAT DOES it look like to drop the story line of "me"? There was a baseball movie out a while back in which a star pitcher is facing a star batter at a crucial point in the game. The pitcher is having a hard time focusing. He's thinking about what would happen if the batter got a hit. He's distracted by the fifty thousand fans shouting and waving.

Then he says to himself, "Clear the mechanism." All of a sudden, the sound level in the movie drops into silence. Even though the fans are still moving and waving, you no longer hear them, the silence reflecting what the pitcher is experiencing as he disengages from his own emotional noise. Then he says to himself, "Now just throw the ball to the catcher, like you've done a million times before."

In "clearing the mechanism" he was turning away from his preoccupation with the mental noise of "me," from his fear-based thoughts about imagined results, about himself as a star, as someone special. Then he could enter the direct experience of simply throwing the ball.

Once we can learn to stop focusing on our own inner noise, we can "clear the mechanism" and drop the story line of "me."

We'll always be conditioned beings living in a conditioned world—meaning we'll always have attachments—but it's possible to learn to relate to the clouds of conditioning as just clouds, and see them more and more within the context of the sky.

. . .

ONE OF OUR strongest attachments is to money, and one of our most confused areas is on the relationship of money to the path of self-discovery. The following story is a good example.

A student asked a spiritual teacher to study with him. The teacher told him that it would cost him five hundred dollars a month. Agreeing to pay, for the next three months the student studied very hard.

But, throughout this whole period he felt more and more angry until one day, in a state of total upset, he went to see the teacher. "I shouldn't have to pay for spiritual practice. Why are you charging me so much money? It's just not right, and I can't study with you under these conditions."

He left the teacher and tried to study on his own. After a while he realized he still needed some guidance, so he found another teacher. In their first meeting, the student told the teacher about how he had become resentful about having to pay the first teacher for practice, even though he had practiced hard. The second teacher replied, "Fine. You can practice with me and we'll see how it goes. You don't have to pay me."

Feeling relieved, the student began studying with his new teacher. But he soon noticed that he wasn't making as much effort as he had before. After several months, the teacher called him in and said, "I think it would be best if you didn't study with me anymore." The student was a little stunned, and asked, "Why, what's the matter?" The teacher responded, "You say you don't think you should pay for practice, yet your behavior shows that you're not willing to practice seriously unless you pay money for it."

. . .

How can this story help us understand our own situation? Does it point to our pictures of the relationship of money to our spiritual quest? On the one hand, it may often seem that money and spirituality don't mix; conversely, we often place value on something in proportion to how much we pay for it.

Money issues, along with sexual issues, obviously play a dominant role in everyday life, yet we rarely consider either of these issues in terms of spiritual practice. Money issues tend to be seen as not even worthy of "spiritual" considerations. But given how much of our daily life distress is related to finances, it is unfortunate that we tend to overlook this crucial area of practice.

Money issues make an especially rich field for practice because our relationship to money is predominantly determined by unconscious beliefs and behaviors. Money issues are rarely just about money.

We have to come back again and again to the point of practice. The point of practice is freedom—freedom from the constraint of *all* of our views, our strategies, our attachments.

What good is it, for example, to sit in meditation having great experiences, only to plunge into the anxiety about our financial situation as soon as our meditation ends? "Practice" includes everything, even the mundane world of money. Until we are free from our deep-seated beliefs about money, as well as our deeply conditioned behaviors, we cannot truly be free.

What's the practice here? It has to begin with observing our believed thoughts around money in order to know what we're up to. We can begin to discover them by asking ourselves questions such as the following: Do I experience tightness and anxiety around money issues?

Do I sense the loss of control, the fear of chaos, of danger, of doom?

If so, what strategy do I fall into—excessive frugality, frantic obsessing, withdrawal into hopelessness? How much of this strategy is based primarily on fear-based projections that have almost no relationship to what's actually happening right now?

The more we observe ourselves, the more it becomes clear that there are many "me's," who often contradict each other. Some of us hold the perhaps unconscious view that money is somehow impure, at the same time valuing things only in terms of what we pay for them.

What's important is to bring precision to our self-observation in order to clearly label what we're actually thinking. Some examples: "Once I get my money situation under control I'll be safe and able to relax." "I'll never be able to take care of myself." "It's better to spend in a carefree manner and have fun than it is to be uptight and frugal." "It's better to be frugal than to be careless about spending and about the future."

Each of these examples not only indicates a different belief in relation to money, but also points to a particular set of strategies about how to cope with life. And with each belief and strategy that we blindly hold to, we restrict and narrow our life. It's only through endlessly *seeing* into our beliefs and behaviors that our attachment to money can be uncovered.

WE DON'T HAVE to set up a new ideal about how to be; we just need to clearly see what we do.

14

IDEALS

There's a famous story about a spiritual master who was falsely accused of sexual misconduct —of fathering the child of a local peasant woman. When presented with this accusation, as well as with the child, he simply said, "Let it be so," and took the child under his care. Sometime later, after feeling guilt and remorse, the mother came to the master and confessed the truth, begging for her child back. Again, he replied, "Let it be so," and returned the child he had helped raise to its mother. I don't know if this story is true, but it certainly portrays an ideal of non-attachment that we can all aspire to. The problem, of course, is when we turn the ideal into something to use against ourselves, to judge ourselves as lacking and unworthy. There is a big difference between having an ideal that inspires us and seeing the ideal as a rigid expectation that we must measure up to.

The one easy way to spot these ideals is to look closely at emotional upsets around one's practice. Emotional distress is a certain sign that we're experiencing life through the filter of an ideal, a picture, or an expectation.

In such a situation, we need only ask the question, "*How is it supposed to be?*" The question will point us to what pictures and requirements we're living from. The practice is to keep seeing how the pictures prevent us from being with what *is*.

Then, with the question "How is it *really*?" we return to our experience itself.

When I was six years old, I lived in an apartment house on the boardwalk in Atlantic City, New Jersey. My father owned a retail store about two miles down the boardwalk. During the tourist season he would work fourteen hours a day. Since he couldn't come home for supper, every night my mother would make him a hot meal and put it in a brown paper bag. My job was to carry this bag in the basket of my tricycle and deliver it to my father while it was still hot. I can still see myself—a very earnest little boy single-mindedly speeding down the boardwalk on my tricycle so that my father could have a hot supper.

There's no doubt that I felt a natural desire to do good, but somewhere along the line, perhaps from repeatedly being praised as a "good boy," my natural desire to do good became enmeshed with getting my father's approval and love.

Many of us have our own version of this syndrome because when we're children, we're naturally attuned to doing whatever it takes to ensure the approval and love of our caregivers. But the problem arises when we're adults living out of the same old pictures—particularly of how we *should* be—without awareness of what's behind our need to help.

Are we helping out of a sense of "should"?

Do we need to be seen as a helper?

Can we see how attached we are to our self-image, our identity?

Who would we be without it?

What hole are we trying to fill with it?

Most of our life is spent living out of behavioral strategies meant to cover or avoid our pain—the deep sense of basic alienation that takes the form of feeling worthless or fundamentally flawed in some way. When our strategy is to help, when we *need* to be helpful, this requires that we find people who seem helpless, or situations that seem to require help.

It's true that we may also have a genuine desire to help—one that isn't based on *our* needs—but whenever we feel an urgency or longing to help, it's often rooted in our fears of facing our own unhealed pain.

If our basic fear is that we'll always be alone, what better way to avoid it than to find someone who needs us? If we have an underlying feeling of worthlessness, how better to prove that we're worthy than by being a helper doing good deeds?

I WAS a hospice volunteer for a ten-year period in my fifties and sixties. When I was assigned my first patient, Richard, a fifty-two-year-old with terminal brain cancer, I was still experiencing discomfort and self-doubt about what to actually do when with someone who was terminally ill. So, I decided to get acquainted briefly with Richard a few days before making my first hospice visit. Although I made this unofficial visit on the pretext of making Richard feel more comfortable, in truth it was to make *me* feel more comfortable.

His wife answered the door and took me to meet her husband, who was standing in a dark hallway. After speaking for a minute in a friendly way, Richard blurted out, "It's hopeless!" and walked into his room, closing the door. As I turned to his wife, she said, "I'm terrified," and started to cry. She quickly walked away from me, and not knowing what to do, I left the house. I was so stunned by what had happened that all I could do was sit in my car for a while.

When I got home, I called my hospice supervisor, who tried to reassure me. I meditated a lot over the next few days, trying to ground myself, but the anxiety and self-doubt remained. By the time I returned to Richard's house I was braced for the worst, with a variety of contingency plans. But when his wife answered the door with a smile and took me in to see Richard, who was cheerfully watching wrestling on television, I was thrown almost as off-balance as on the first visit.

In both cases I had gone in with expectations—based entirely on mental pictures—of who to be and what to do. That I needed to be open to change, to the unexpected, without the illusion that I, "the hospice helper," could substantially control or change anything, is a lesson I learned over and over again, not just from patient to patient, but from one visit to the next. Often conditions were changing so rapidly that they could never be pinned down with some set expectation of what should happen.

This meant giving up the comfort of my familiar identities, of who to be and what to do. Without dropping my identity as "the helper" and my mental picture of the patient as someone to be helped, I would never have been able to connect in a meaningful way.

. . .

In fact, as we try to fulfill our pictures of how we should be, we may also see that we can really do very little to change substantially. We make New Year's resolutions, we go on diets, we say we'll meditate every day, we try not to be defensive, we try to be nice and patient, but almost always we experience the disappointment and futility of this approach. Trying to change our behavior just doesn't seem to work, as the history of moralistic religion and the cultures associated with it have clearly demonstrated.

Once we see this, disappointment rather than moral dictate becomes our best teacher. Instead of trying to change our behavior, we realize the sanity of learning to be with our life as it is—thus allowing transformation to evolve on its own.

PART II

15

KINDNESS

"Before you know what kindness really is
you must lose things, feel the future
dissolve in a moment..." —Naomi Shihab Nye

SEVERAL YEARS AGO, toward the end of my teaching career at a Zen meditation center, two students filed a civil suit against both me and the meditation center. I had taught for over twenty-three years without anything like this ever happening, and because I knew I didn't do what I was charged with, I was shocked that something like it could occur. Ultimately the civil suit was dismissed and I was acquitted of all the claims, but the sorrow and disappointment that I felt—in being judged and dismissed by people I cared about—went very deep.

Up until that point, I felt that our position at the center was very stable. But it soon became clear, once again, that we are all skating on thin ice. Anything can happen out of the blue. It's not a question of fair or unfair; it's just part of the unpredictability of life.

I learned once again that to rely on reputation for one's happiness is like building a foundation on sand. Our reputation is external to us; it is not about who we are but how we're seen by others. We can do little to control it; it can be taken away without warning, or unfairly, with no recourse for getting it back. In this instance I could "feel the future dissolve in a moment."

This became especially clear when the civil suit became public. The way the charges were worded made me sound really bad, and regardless of the fact that I didn't do what I was charged with, the mark on my reputation was irreparable.

I could have chosen to write a rebuttal. Or complain. Or blame. Or wallow in self-pity. But what would have been the point? On the path of self-realization, any of those choices would have been a dead end, and only added more suffering to the situation. Much better to rely on knowing who I was in the larger sense, including knowing that our time is limited.

So even though my mind wanted to fight the misrepresentations, my heart told me to let it be. I chose to accept what my life was in that very disappointing situation. This meant being willing to feel the humiliation of seeing a condemning mark placed on my reputation. It also meant having to feel the sadness of losing connection with some people I cared about.

THERE'S no question that I felt anger. And betrayal. But I kept reminding myself of the legend of the monk who, when presented with the baby that wasn't his, simply said, "Let it be so" and took the baby as his own. I couldn't say "Let it be so" very easily, but the story reminded me to breathe my distressing feelings right into the center of my chest and really feel them physically.

I also tried to keep remembering a quote from the Stoic philosopher Epictetus: "What really frightens and dismays us is not external events themselves, but the way in which we think about them. It is not things that disturb us, but our interpretation of their significance."

What became most clear to me was how attached I was to my self-image. But staying with the feelings and breathing into the heart allowed me to free myself increasingly of that attachment. It also allowed me to internally process the messiness of the group dynamics that I had witnessed, as well as the self-righteous certainty from some people I had once trusted.

PRACTICING LOVING KINDNESS WAS KEY. I had been doing a version of the loving kindness meditation for many years, and the emphasis was not on trying to feel a particular way, such as loving or kind; rather, the focus was on following the breath into the center of the chest while paying particular attention to what blocks our natural kindness from coming forth.

I began doing the loving kindness meditation toward each person I felt had turned against me, and toward whom I felt anger. As I said, a crucial part of the loving kindness meditation (which is included at the end of this chapter) is to pay attention to whatever blocks kindness and love within oneself. Although it took a while, my anger gave way to insight into the layers of hurt, grief, and fear underneath the anger. Feeling my own pain also allowed me to see and feel the pain of those who I felt had acted harmfully toward me. I saw how unnecessary it was to feel like I was right, and what a waste of time it was trying to prove my case.

As the need to self-justify faded, I began to feel deep remorse for the pain and suffering that this incident triggered in others. Many in the community were caught in the confusion of not knowing the facts of what really happened. But I was still surprised to see how ready some of the people were to judge me. Because I knew I was innocent of the charges, the ability to feel deep remorse for the people involved was not an easy place to reach. Again, doing the loving kindness meditation was crucial. Ultimately, the warmth I felt for others felt much more genuine than my anger at believing I was falsely accused and judged.

ONE THING I learned is that we can never tell what will come our way, however unfair; nor can we know what others will do in any given situation. But most of all I understood more deeply that my kindness toward others couldn't depend on how others were treating me, or on how I was feeling in the moment. This is where genuine kindness began to shine through. As I stayed with my life exactly as it was, I was able to see and experience the depth of my own unkindness, as it had manifested in my anger and resentment toward others. Paradoxically, the willingness to look at and attend to my own unkindness is what ultimately helped it heal and transform into real kindness, as well as a sense of inner freedom.

"HISTORY IS NOT JUST facts and events. History is also a pain in the heart, and we repeat history until we are able to make another's pain in the heart our own." —Julius Lester

16

LOVING KINDNESS MEDITATION

Take a couple of deep breaths. Become aware of the breath and begin to follow it into the center of the chest, relaxing into the body.

WHATEVER YOU FEEL, just be aware of that. With each in-breath, let awareness go a little deeper.

TO ACTIVATE the quality of kindness, first think of someone for whom you have very positive feelings. Picture them. Breathe them in. Let your innate kindness be activated.

TO ONESELF: Stay with each line for a few breaths.

"Breathing in, dwelling in the heart.
Breathing out, extending kindness to myself,
exactly as I am right now."

. . .

Relating with a benign friendliness to whatever you're feeling, basically wishing yourself well. If there is no warmth, no kindness to extend, simply notice this, and continue.

"Breathing in, dwelling in the heart.
Breathing out, attending to whatever
blocks kindness and love."

Noticing wherever you are caught in self-judgment or anger or closed-heartedness, letting awareness heal.

"Breathing in, dwelling in the heart.
Breathing out, extending kindness to others."

Feeling the generosity of the heart in extending kindness to others. Repeat the above lines one or two more times.

TO OTHERS: Now think of someone close to you, for whom you wish to extend kindness. Breathe the person's image into the center of the chest on the in-breath.

On the out-breath, extend kindness to this person while repeating the lines. Stay with each line for a few rounds of the breath.

"Breathing (name) in, dwelling in the heart.
Breathing out, extending kindness to (name),
exactly as you are right now."

Wishing for them a benign friendliness to wherever they're at right now.

"Breathing (name) in, dwelling in the heart.
Breathing out, may you be healed in your difficulties."

. . .

Basically wishing that they learn, and perhaps become free, of their difficulties.

"Breathing (name) in, dwelling in the heart.
Breathing out, may you extend kindness to others."

Wishing for them to be able to feel for the well-being of everyone. You can repeat these lines to as many others as you wish.

Initially there may be some discomfort in doing the loving kindness meditation, including a lot of resistance. However, no matter what you experience—whether it is awkwardness, resistance, or skepticism—it is well worth it to keep practicing the meditation, and to give it a chance by doing it daily if at all possible.

As we do the loving kindness meditation on a regular basis, it is no longer just a meditation exercise; it becomes more a part of who we are, where kindness increasingly becomes our natural response to ourselves and to others.

"Be kind whenever possible. It's always possible." —Dalai Lama

17

SUFFERING AND GRACE

Our unkindness, and all of our suffering, is the direct consequence of wanting our life to be other than it is.

SEVERAL YEARS AGO, in my role as a hospice volunteer, I met Robert, a forty-seven-year-old man who was dying of cancer, with a variety of serious complications. When I met him for the first time, he was lying asleep in his bed. His face was pale and gaunt and he looked almost dead. Above the bed hung a large picture of him and his wife dancing on their wedding day. He looked so vibrant and happy in his white tuxedo, so very different from how he looked now.

When we met, I was at the beginning stage of what was to be an acute and prolonged relapse into an immune system disease I had had for some time. As a result, when Robert and I began to talk that first day, we connected deeply and immediately. Neither of us held back, neither of us was interested in presenting the usual pretentions, neither of us was trying to protect ourself from the painful feelings that we were both experiencing.

We were able to just meet and share our fears, but without the usual melodrama. We didn't talk about anything "spiritual"; he didn't have a concept about dying "consciously," and I didn't make any suggestions to him on how to practice with his difficult situation.

His main concern was to make a video, a visual memory for his five-year-old daughter. But he was very weak and in considerable pain. On subsequent visits he mentioned that he was even considering suicide. He said he just wanted his suffering to end.

I visited him several times, for just a few hours, and we continued to have a strong and honest connection. Then, because my own health was rapidly declining, I couldn't visit anymore. Instead, we spoke on the phone, continuing to share openly. As we talked about our mutual sense of grief and loss, I began to detect a shift in Robert. He no longer spoke of suicide. Even though his body was rapidly declining, we talked more about our connection; within our shared pain there was also a sense of shared heart. Within what appeared to be separate individual suffering we found connectedness.

Robert knew that my immune system had been undermined by prolonged exposure to pesticides. One day he called to tell me about a remedy that might help me detoxify. Listening to him talk, I was thinking, "He's probably going to die any day now—why is he calling me to help with *my* difficulties?"

His last word to me, which echoed in my mind as I put the phone down, was "*Sayonara*." When he died the next day, I wondered if he knew he was saying goodbye.

I found out later that he'd called a few people that day, trying to reach out, to give something back. That's what he chose to do on the last day of his life. Here was a person who had real difficulties, and he didn't want the pain and suffering any more than the rest of us. In fact, at one point, he was ready to end his life on his own.

Yet something transformed. He willingly surrendered to his life as it was. He then experienced a grace made possible by learning to bear the unbearable. He learned to say Yes to life and to give something back.

WE MAY NOT BE FORCED to face our suffering through circumstances as intense as Robert's, but all of us have our own measure of difficulty with which we have to deal. How willing we are to learn from our suffering will determine the quality of our life.

How deeply we understand what it means to trust in, to reside in, whatever comes to us—especially the unpleasant and the unwanted—is the key to opening into genuine appreciation and joy.

Yes, we will confuse this issue and distort the practice; yes, we will resist our lives in endless ways; but gradually, with perseverance, we will also begin to learn. We can't simply stop confusing, distorting, and resisting, but we can learn to see what we do.

It's this seeing that allows us to gradually reside directly in the bodily experience we call suffering. Only then can we understand that what we call joy is simply the willingness to be truly present with what is—including, and especially, the suffering that none of us wants.

18

GRIEF

Sometimes, especially with loss, we cannot avoid experiencing suffering, especially grief.

Grief arises through many situations, not only when someone we love dies. Those who have experienced divorce have felt grief, as anger over the dissolution of ideals, or sadness at the loss of a sacred bond. Those who have lost faith in their religion, especially after relying on it for support, have experienced grief, perhaps felt as emptiness and groundlessness.

Anyone who has seen their heroes or idols falter has experienced the feelings of sadness and incompleteness that are part of grief. When someone we love or admire dies, often our grief is more about ourselves than for a lost person—for the expectations and dreams that might never be fulfilled.

Often, when we are grieving for someone or something we have lost, we feel the pain and sadness of separation. We can feel it as an ache, as a tightness in the throat, as a hole in the center of the chest.

Often fears are invoked—of isolation, of emptiness, of

the unknown. And almost always there is the insecurity of losing an anchor, the feeling of groundlessness that comes when we feel there is nothing to hold onto.

When the pain of loss arises, we always have the choice to try to ward it off, bury it, or finally let it in. Considering the many faces of grief, it's no wonder that we so often choose to push it away. Not only is it difficult to make sense of loss, it's even more difficult to allow ourselves to feel the intense and often unpleasant sensations that follow.

The fact is: we cannot avoid pain and grief, but we can avoid indulging in them.

I'm in my late seventies, so it's natural that many people in my life have already died. The deaths that affected me the most were five of my closest friends, including my former wife—all of whom died relatively young. Two of them died in their forties, suddenly and with no warning. I had known one of them since kindergarten; we went through school together, were college roommates for four years, and later I built a home for him and his family. Then shortly after he turned forty, he took his own life, and when I heard the news, I was so shaken that I broke down every day, sometimes uncontrollably, for several weeks.

In part, my grieving was the realization of how much pain he had to be in to do what he did. But a large part of it, I realized later, was not just for the loss of someone I cared deeply about—but for something inside of me that seemed to have gotten lost as well. My (not necessarily conscious) view of the world was that there was a stability and certainty that I could count on. There was also the belief (again not conscious) that I myself had endless time. My friend's death shattered these illusions, and the sense of groundlessness shook my feelings of complacency.

But as intense as my feelings were, after a time my former sense of control returned, although now with a little less certainty. My other friend who died young had been my closest friend for twenty-five years; he was the one person I could talk to about anything and feel understood. In his late forties, he had a sudden and massive heart attack while playing basketball. He died instantly, and when I was given the news, I was unable to even take it in. At the time, I was in the middle of a several-months-long acute flare-up of an autoimmune disorder. I didn't have the energy or strength to process the feelings, so for two months, until I started to get better, I buried them. Then, as my strength returned, the deep waves of sadness and loss rose to the surface. Fortunately, by then I was able to process the grief in a way that deepened my heart, and also connected me more deeply with the grief that we all share.

I learned that even though someone dies, they still can have a very profound place in the heart. For many years after his death, I silently talked to him every day—sharing my life with him as if he were still there. It's not that I believed he could literally hear me; it was more the sense of connectedness that survives the loss of the body.

EACH EXPERIENCE of grief has hit me differently. I was with my mother in the hospital when she was diagnosed with lymphoma, with a poor prognosis. While I was there, I was able to maintain a calm presence for her, but as soon as I left the hospital it felt like I had been punched in the stomach. I remember having to lean against the brick wall of the hospital—the same building where I had been born fifty-three years earlier—and feeling like my tether to the earth was being disconnected.

There's no way to prepare for an experience like that; as with aging, we're all beginners when it comes to dealing with grief. We may not even know what we're feeling or what to do with it.

Grief is difficult to feel because it's often both intense and constantly changing. Sometimes it manifests as anger, sometimes as fear, often as sadness and dread. Sometimes grief arises at the most seemingly unlikely times—when we hear a bird singing or see a flower in bloom. Often one small moment of grief taps into other griefs—the layers of unresolved pain that we've been avoiding—such as fears of separation, abandonment, and insecurity.

From my own experiences and also from working with others, I've learned that there's no way to truly anticipate the intensity of the feelings of grief. When someone we love dies, the loss can sometimes seem unbearable. The closer we are, especially when we have become "glued at the hip" to one another, the more painful the loss. Often the mind cannot accept it—the belief that "This was not supposed to happen!" can stay with us for weeks and even months or years. The days can seem empty; the thought of tomorrow or next week can leave us feeling numb or disheartened; birthdays, holidays, and particularly anniversaries can make us feel raw all over again.

. . .

For a time, grief can become our whole existence—the feelings of pain and emptiness may be all that we know. But over time, we usually gain some distance from our feelings, particularly as we allow the feelings to pass through the heart. The intensity begins to lessen, and sometimes we even forget we're grieving. Then at times it may come back full bore.

Someone described this experience as being like the ocean, with the waves of grief at first being large and frequent, pushing us down to the ocean floor. Unable to hold our breath, it feels as if we will drown. Then the waves subside, and we can come up for air. As time passes, so do the currents, and the waves become smaller and less frequent, although occasionally a large wave will come out of nowhere and knock us back down again. But by then we have learned that we will not drown.

When our grief is very strong, we often turn to culturally acceptable ways to avoid feeling the pain. Perhaps we adopt a feeling of martyred nobility in "my suffering." We might force ourselves to "be strong," or grieve "in the right way." Perhaps, as spiritual practitioners, we even invoke the perspective of the Absolute, pretending to understand that "God works in mysterious ways," or that "life and death are one."

But invoking these *as attitudes*—without the inner understanding—or taking *any* position that prevents us from honestly facing what's really going on is just another way of burying grief. It's one more way of erecting armor to avoid exposing our heart to fear and pain.

We also cut ourselves off from our true feelings when we offer platitudes to someone in grief. It is often very difficult to know what to say or do with someone who has just lost a loved one. Although we might hide behind phrases like "It will get better with time" or "They're in a better place," phrases like these often make the grieving person feel worse.

Better to just let them know you care about them, and that you will be there for them.

BUT EXPOSURE TO LOSS, especially when it involves the death of someone we love, also has the power to awaken aspiration as few other circumstances can. Death, serious illness, or injury can jolt us straight into reality. Suddenly we see how much of our life is wasted on trivialities; we understand to what degree we're just skating on thin ice; we appreciate that time is swiftly passing, and with it, our only chance of awakening to a genuine life.

Our suffering does not have to turn into hopelessness or doom as long as we remember that it's our teacher. We also have to remember that the willingness to open to life's difficulties does not depend on liking them.

Rethinking our priorities is the beginning of opening into loss. We're no longer so intent on clinging to our protections. We're no longer so interested in preserving comfort and safety as our gods. We begin to feel the pettiness of our attitudes and opinions. We begin to feel the magnitude of holding our hearts back in fear.

At this point, when our priorities have been turned right-side-up, we become more willing to allow the intensity of loss into our experience. But how do we do this? How can we best open into loss?

. . .

The practice of opening into loss involves bringing awareness into a point directly in the center of the chest, sometimes called the "grief point." In the intensity of grief this point is sometimes so sensitive that when we press it with our fingers, we can feel the tenderness.

In this practice, first we bring awareness to the experience of loss as it manifests in the body. Perhaps we feel it as heaviness, an ache, or as tightness in the throat. Breathing into the center of the chest, we breathe the sensations of loss directly into the heart space. On the out-breath, we softly release.

We're not trying to do anything with our experience of loss other than let it in. We're not trying to transform it. We're not trying to let it go. Rather, by breathing it into the center of the chest we're inviting ourselves to experience it in a new way, within the context of the spaciousness of the heart, beyond thinking.

Recently, two close friends were very ill with cancer. Quite concerned that they would die soon, I was feeling sad and heavy. I wasn't even aware of how caught up I was in believed thoughts of doom, such as "Life is just too hard." But as soon as I remembered to begin breathing into the center of the chest, pulling the heaviness and the gloom directly into the heart space, my experience of loss changed dramatically. Breathing into the chest center undercut the thoughts, and after only a few minutes of residing in the heart of the experience, my heaviness lifted.

What remained was simply the sadness—but it was sadness without the heaviness, without the believed thoughts, without the melodrama. And within the sadness was also an openness to life and a profound sense of connection with my friends. It felt like a much more genuine and authentic response to the moment.

In practicing with loss, it's possible to work very specifically, step by step, with the conditions and attachments that intensify our emotional reactions. In fact, there's a very useful meditation practice that helps bring clarity to the process of grief even when there are no external catastrophes.

I learned a version of this practice when I was training to be a hospice volunteer, and found it so powerful that I've continued doing it in a modified form ever since.

I have twenty small cards, and on each one I've written either the name of someone I am very close to, or one of my closely held identities (teacher, writer, etc.), or one of my favorite activities (nature walking, athletics, etc.), or some other important aspect of my life (good health, material security, etc.).

These are my strongest attachments, and therefore the places where my expectations and emotional loads are heaviest. Every couple of weeks, I sit down with the twenty cards in my hands. With my eyes closed, I shuffle them while I begin breathing into the center of the chest.

When I feel settled, I thumb through the cards until my fingers come to rest on a specific one. I ask myself, "What would it be like if I were to never have this in my life again?" Opening my eyes and reading the card, I try to feel what it would be like to experience the loss. At the same time, I stay aware of breathing in and out of the chest center.

When it's a person's name on the card, I make a real effort to see her as dead. I imagine not being able to ever see her or talk to her again. I picture the specific situations in which I presently have contact with the person, and imagine the same situations without her. In short, I try to make this exercise as real as possible in order to actually feel the pain of loss.

You may wonder: Why would anyone want to engage in such a seemingly morose preoccupation with personal suffering? While it's true that this exercise can bring up some intense and unpleasant feelings, its purpose is quite the opposite of perpetuating suffering. It allows us to clearly see and experience the roots of much of our pain: our expectations, our requirements, our attachments, and our cherished opinions.

In exploring these roots, in experiencing the conditions out of which most of our suffering arises, we can gradually become freer of them. And unlike a real-life situation, where the shock of loss can overwhelm our ability to deal with it, this exercise is done within the more controlled environment of meditation.

Once, when doing this exercise, one of my daughters' names came up. I immediately put the card down and got up and walked away. It just seemed like too much to deal with. But later I came back to the card and did the exercise with her name. It was difficult, but as I stayed with it, I began to see how I had petty and unnecessary requirements of her—requirements that got in the way of love. As I dropped the requirements, I felt a much deeper appreciation for her.

Imagining someone we love as dead, it's possible to see clearly how unimportant most of our requirements and agendas are. This visualization could enable us to more deeply appreciate the people and things we love. The Stoics, who also practiced imagining a loved one as dead, believed that we are less likely to take someone for granted if we are aware that they may not be in our life forever.

It is true that we are essentially alone, and that we die alone. But to die alone does not mean we die in loneliness. Awareness is what heals. Awareness is what allows us to experience our basic connectedness with everyone and everything.

19

WORKING WITH ANGER

Many practitioners on the path of self-realization get discouraged when they realize how difficult it is to maintain an aware and awake state. Quite often, even after a good period of meditation or yoga first thing in the morning, where we feel somewhat aware and awake, we may "come to" later in the day with the realization that we've since spent hours in a state of "waking sleep."

The question is: Why is it so hard to awaken? In part, it's because the life force, or energy, necessary to awaken is constantly leaking away from morning till night.

Perhaps the most significant leak occurs through the manifestation of negative emotions, where energy is squandered in small and sometimes huge doses throughout the day. Negative, as used here, simply means an emotion that negates or denies. It says "No" to life. Anger, for example, says, "I don't want this!"

This does not apply only to loud outbursts of anger. We manifest negative emotions, in smaller doses, all day long: as irritability, judgments of self and others, impatience, passive aggression, and so on.

One important emphasis is learning what closes these leaks. This is why we must pay attention to how to work with our negative emotions, particularly the many forms of anger. An analogy used earlier might be helpful in understanding this process: We all know that food provides energy for the body. But there's another kind of "food," namely our impressions or experience, that feeds our *Being*.

Every experience, much like the food we consume, can either nourish or deplete us, depending on how much awareness is present and what our intention is. When we react to an experience negatively, it's like eating bad food. It doesn't digest. In fact, it can even poison us. When that happens, we often spew the poison back out into the world, usually at another person.

The alternative to manifesting negative emotions is to bring awareness to the actual energy of the reaction—the physical experience itself. Normally, we fuel our reactions by believing and justifying the thoughts that accompany them. But when we disengage from this pattern, attention can instead be focused on the visceral experience of the emotion.

This attention allows a different type of digestion to take place. For example, when we can stop the *expression* of anger and instead *experience* its actual energy, that raw energy may transform into nourishment on our path to self-realization.

I'M NOT SUGGESTING that negative emotions should not arise, nor that we should repress them. The instruction is simply to refrain from *expressing* them, either outwardly through words and actions, or inwardly through spinning and obsessive thoughts. It is only through the process of not expressing negative emotions and actually *experiencing* their energy that we learn to live in accord with our true nature, our natural kindness.

If we could see our angry emotional reactions clearly, it would become obvious how they deplete our energy and consequently narrow our life. We would also see how, when we're caught in anger, we're cut off from the heart, from a sense of our basic connectedness.

For example, when someone swerves in front of me on the freeway, anger arises in a microsecond, and I may get caught in the strong impulse to yell and gesture. I will certainly feel justified in being irate. But what happens if, instead of expressing the anger, I simply stay with the visceral experience?

Practicing in this way over time teaches us to connect more deeply with our experience, and finally we are able to recognize the situation as it is—that another car/driver simply cut us off, and that is all. Perhaps we can also label the reactions we have as just believed thoughts, such as, "Having a believed thought that he's a moron," "Having a believed thought that she shouldn't be allowed to drive," or "Having a believed thought that this always happens to me."

As we learn to see our reactions more clearly, and to label the thoughts associated with them, we become more and more capable of experiencing our anger as just what is—heat in our face or tension in our muscles and gut. We might even see that what really happened is that we simply got scared. Above all, we no longer hold onto our emotions and thoughts as the objective truth about what actually happened.

At a certain point, in addition to experiencing our

emotions and labeling our thoughts, we may even feel compassion—in this example, for the driver who cut us off; or, at least we might laugh at ourselves for getting so worked up over an objectively small or insignificant occurrence.

The point is, when we don't express anger, not only is the energy leakage closed, but the very energy that would have leaked away also becomes available for nourishing a genuine reconnection with life.

THERE'S A VERY instructive story about Gandhi, who was about to lead a march protesting the British monopoly on sea salt. There were tens of thousands of his followers waiting on the beach to begin the march, but Gandhi realized he was still very angry at the British, and didn't want to lead while in that state. He went in his tent and meditated for hours, even knowing his followers were waiting for him. Finally, he came out, but now he was free from his anger and felt that he could connect with followers and lead in good conscience.

ONE COMMON POINT of confusion relating to this process is misunderstanding the difference between non-expression and *suppression.* When anger is suppressed, it means that we are not feeling it. This can be particularly problematic for meditators who have been brought up suppressing their anger, because they can easily mistake their suppression for spiritual maturity. But suppressed anger tends to fester; the poisonous energy of anger can even pollute the body, often impacting our physical health.

When we instead withhold the expression of anger, it

is very different from suppression. Non-expression actually allows us to feel—to fully feel—the emotion of anger directly, letting it simply be there without needing to do anything about it. This is how our anger naturally heals.

So why is it so difficult to stop the expression of anger? We seem to hold onto this habit with a stubbornness that defies all sense. The simple answer is: we *want* to be angry. We want to be right. This may not always be obvious, but the feelings of juiciness and power that can accompany the expression of anger are often intoxicating.

Rage gives us a false feeling of power and control, but is always a way of avoiding feeling the fear of powerlessness that we don't want to feel.

This all makes sense from an evolutionary point of view, where raw instinctual reactions once served a real purpose: they allowed our ancestors to ward off physical threats in order to survive. However, even though we no longer face the same kinds of danger, and thus no longer need the same kind of response, our bodies and minds have not yet caught on. So that juicy, "good" feeling of anger remains, though it no longer serves us, particularly if we are on the path of trying to live a more harmonious life.

THERE IS another important reason why we may choose to stay angry. Expressing negative emotions can cover over the fear-based pain that often underlies our anger—the pain that we simply don't want to feel.

For example, we will often feel an immediate surge of anger when we are criticized. Most of the time, we will jump directly into blaming and self-justifying, which is our automatic defense mechanism or protective strategy for avoiding feeling the pain of rejection and unworthiness that the criticism triggers. But if instead we refrain from expressing anger, we can go deeper into our experience and truly *feel* not only the energy of anger itself, but also the core of pain beneath it.

A while back, I was publicly denounced. Even though I knew the criticisms were untrue, I was still publicly humiliated and really angry about it. I found myself mentally and physically agitated, and heard my mind repeating my self-justifications as well as blaming the people I felt were at fault. When I realized how I was stuck in my story line of anger and blame, I began the practice of silently saying "Don't go there!" every time I would find myself caught in the mental spinning.

I think the first few days I must have used this expression hundreds of times, but each time I used it I would turn my attention away from the story and toward the physical experience of anger itself—the heat, the agitation, the contraction. And as I stayed with my visceral experience, it slowly became clear that what I was feeling most deeply was hurt and fear and sadness. The anger dissipated and what remained was a heaviness in the center of my chest.

And as I breathed into my chest, it felt like sunshine and fresh air began to permeate the experience. Over the next weeks the anger and its story line would still pop up now and then, but saying "Don't go there!" would bring me back to simply feeling hurt, with no need to self-justify or blame.

This is often a quiet *inner* process, where we stay intently present with our experience in a way that allows us to break through layers and layers of protective armoring. We thereby enter into the fear-based pain we've never wanted to feel; and while it is never pleasant to be with our most deep-seated pain and fear, it is only by uncovering and residing in this place that true transformation can occur. Only here can we ultimately reconnect with our basic wholeness.

Remember, when we feel that others have hurt us, our usual tendency is to get angry and then to judge and blame them. We are also rarely aware that our blaming is mainly an attempt to cover our own pain, including the pain of seeing ourselves as diminished, or as not enough in some way. So, we get angry or resentful, and then focus on the shortcomings of those who have hurt us.

But in our blaming, there is another subtle dynamic going on. When we take offense at others, we think our offense or hurt is the result of what they did or didn't do. We thus use *their* behavior to justify *our* anger. But in so doing, we're missing a crucial point: when we get caught in blame and justification—in our anger and resentment—we have lost our own way. We have cut ourselves off from the heart, from the love and connection that is our true nature.

Such situations may, in fact, eventually require taking objective steps to remedy potentially harmful outward actions. Fortunately, transforming the negative energy of anger by working with it inwardly can give us a strong sense of resolve, which we can then use to address, in a positive way, whatever may need to be done.

As Martin Luther King said: "Our lives begin to end the day we become silent about things that matter." But no longer being silent first requires that we resolve the negativity of anger within ourselves.

In other words, the real transformative process is an inner one. We have to acknowledge that it is our *own* darkness that has pulled us off the path, not the darkness of the other. Even though the other may have done something unskillful or unkind, this *never* justifies our unkindness in return.

The Stoic philosopher Seneca observed: "Whatever one of us blames in another, each one will find in his own heart."

Though something in us already *knows* this, it often takes only a nanosecond to go from this innate understanding to the mental realm of judging and blaming the other.

Sadly, it is from our own unkindness toward the other, as manifested in our judging and blaming, that we make the choice to live from a closed heart. And in so doing, we are choosing to live as a victim, insisting on being right, and elevating ourselves by putting the other down.

Practicing with anger ultimately allows us to see that when people treat us unkindly, it is *their* action, born of *their* suffering, and has little to do with us. And while we may still want to use their actions to justify our negative reaction, we should be aware that we have another choice; we can instead choose to turn away from blaming,

When we can, in fact, turn away from blaming—which entails a willingness to feel our own anger, hurt, and fear—we open ourselves to relating to the other in a new way. We are now able to *see* them in their all-too-human garb, as just another human being in pain.

Perhaps we may even understand that they were not *trying* to hurt us, but simply acting out of their own pain-induced closed-heartedness. This understanding is the essence of compassion.

When we are no longer under the shadow of anger and resentment, true kindness can arise. Remember: true kindness is never dependent on how others treat us, or on how we may be feeling in the moment.

As Martin Luther King stated: "Returning hate for hate multiplies hate, adding deeper darkness to a night already devoid of stars. Darkness cannot drive out darkness; only light can do that. Hate cannot drive out hate; only love and kindness can do that."

And as the Stoic Seneca observed, "Wherever there is a human being, there is an opportunity for kindness."

20

THE DILEMMA OF FEAR

It is anxiety and fear, perhaps more than anything, that get in the way of experiencing our basic connectedness.

Much of the path of self-discovery is about dealing with fear. Fear tells us to close down, to not go beyond the protective outer edge of our cocoon. But by giving in to fear, we make it more solid. We strengthen our cocoon, contracting and limiting our existence.

Fear has us avoiding some terrible imagined outcome, yet the substitute life we experience by giving in to our fear is already a terrible outcome.

The Tibetan Buddhist teacher Pema Chödrön likens our ego to a room, a protective cocoon we spin exactly as we'd like it. The temperature is always just right, we hear only the music we want to hear, we eat only the food we want to eat, and perhaps best of all, we only allow the people we like into our room. In short, we make our life exactly the way we want it—pleasing, comfortable, and safe.

But when we step outside of the room, what happens?

We meet the messiness of everyday life, particularly the irritating people we're trying to shut out of our room, and all of the difficult and unwanted situations we're trying so hard to avoid. The more we meet this unpleasantness, the more we want to retreat into our room, our protective cocoon. We close the windows and even cover them with bars and shutters. We put special locks on the doors. We do whatever we can to shut life out.

But if we're fortunate, one day we might wake up to the realization that in trying to control our world to make it comfortable and safe, we've narrowed our existence to the point where we're no longer truly living.

This closed-down life is built on the foundation of our desire to avoid our deep core fears—fears of helplessness, of being alone, of being unworthy, of experiencing the anxious quiver of being.

The extent to which we wish to avoid these fears is reflected like a mirror in how we experience our life. They numb us to our desire to live a more genuine life. They block our aspiration to live from our naturally open heart. And consequently, even as we maintain our control strategies, we slowly stagnate in dissatisfaction, frustration, and a sense of disconnectedness. These are the signs that we are living in the self-imposed prison of a life that is not real.

THE MESSAGE OF FEAR: close down and defend. Yet the heart calls us to open up and connect.

Every time we give in to fear, we lose our life.

And most poignant, until we become intimate with our fears, they will always limit our ability to love.

A good friend of mine wrote a science fiction novel that features characters from outer space. Whenever they greet each other, instead of saying "Hello," they say, "Please don't hurt me." Isn't this an accurate description of the subliminal undercurrent of fear that runs our lives?

Considering how much fear we all have, it's a wonder we're not already experts on this subject. But fear is one of the most slippery realms in life, as well as on our spiritual journey. The list of what we're afraid of is very long. But there are three universal fears that all of us will ultimately have to deal with.

THE FIRST, most basic fear is that of losing safety. Because safety is fundamental to our survival, this fear will instinctually be triggered at the first sign of danger or insecurity; the old brain, or limbic system, is inherently wired that way.

This particular fear will also be triggered when we experience pain or discomfort. But in many cases, even when this fear is triggered, there is no real danger to us; in fact, our fears are largely imaginary—that the plane will crash, that we will be criticized, that we're doing it wrong. Yet, until we see this dimension of fear with clarity, we will continue to live with a sense of constriction that can seem daunting.

Insecurity can also manifest as the fear of helplessness, often surfacing as the fear of losing control, the fear of being controlled, the fear of chaos, or even the fear of the unfamiliar.

For example, nearly all of us have experienced the emotion of rage, which is like being swept into a mushroom cloud explosion. Think of all those days where nothing seems to go your way, or even just the last time your TV remote stopped working, and no matter what buttons you pushed, you couldn't get it to do what you wanted. The urge to throw the remote against the wall can feel like angry rage, but as we bring awareness to this experience, we can discover that the feeling of rage is often just an outer explosion that is covering over the quieter inner implosion of feeling powerless.

Rage may give us a feeling of power and control, but how often is it an evasion of the sense of powerlessness that feels so much worse?

We all dread the helplessness of losing control; yet, real freedom lies in recognizing the futility of demanding that life be within our control. Instead, as counterintuitive as it may sound, we must learn the willingness to feel—to say Yes to—the experience of helplessness itself.

This is one of the hidden gifts of serious illness or loss. It pushes us right to our edge, where we may have the good fortune to realize that our only real option is to surrender to our experience and let it just be.

THE SECOND BASIC fear is that of aloneness and disconnection, which can also manifest as the fear of abandonment, loss, or death. On some very basic, yet very deep level, all of us feel fundamentally alone; and until we face this directly, we will fear it.

It's interesting that one of life's most vital lessons is something we are never taught in school: how to be at home with ourselves.

Most people will do almost anything to avoid this fear. Many enter into relationships or engage in affairs. In fact, the extent to which people have affairs is often proportional to the urgency of needing to avoid feeling alone.

Ultimately, however, being willing to let loneliness just be—by truly residing in it—is the only way to transcend it. It's also the only way to develop true intimacy with another, because true intimacy can't be based on neediness, or on the fear of being alone.

The basic fear of aloneness may also include a related anxiety that is not usually recognized: the fear of disconnection—from others as well as from our own heart. This fear penetrates deeper than loneliness, and often manifests as a knotted quiver in the chest or abdomen.

Remember, at bottom, the heart that seeks to awaken, to live genuinely, is more real than anything. It is the nameless drive that calls us to be who we most truly are. When we are not in touch with this, we may feel the existential anxiety of disconnection.

THE THIRD BASIC fear is that of unworthiness. This fear takes many forms, such as the fear that you don't count, the fear of general inadequacy, of being unworthy of love, of being nothing or stupid, and so on.

The basic fear that we'll never measure up dictates much of our behavior; for example, for some, it impels us to continuously and forcefully prove ourselves, while for others, it might prompt us to cease trying. In either case, isn't our motivation the same—to avoid facing the basic fear of unworthiness? We may fear the feeling of unworthiness more than anything.

In order to effectively work with our fears, we have to gradually become aware of how much fear there is in almost everything we do—the fear in our ambition, in our depression, the fear behind much of what we call kindness, and of course in our anger. We could even define anger as inexperienced fear.

In my late forties, I had a telling insight into my early relationship with inexperienced fear. As I was listening to an "oldie but goodie" from the early sixties, I had a nice, bittersweet feeling of nostalgia. But in the middle of this nostalgia, I felt an agitation in the pit of my stomach that I recognized as anxiety. I thought, "Why would I have anxiety remembering my teenage years—my 'Golden Age'—when everything was supposedly great?"

Then I realized that I was remembering, *on a cellular level* just from hearing this song, something that was happening within me all along: anxiety. This anxiety was probably motivating me, throughout my teenage years, to frantically have fun and seek diversions. But I wasn't the least bit aware of it then.

It was not until my early twenties that I started becoming acutely aware of my fear. My response: to try to get rid of it. Seeing my fears and how they were constricting my life, I took the time-honored path of trying to eliminate them—to confront them, to struggle with them, to overcome them and become free.

Such a noble and worthy enterprise! Yet because this approach is often the result of our typical upside-down way of thinking, the practice of confronting our fears in the hope of getting rid of them is usually limited and misdirected.

Since I didn't know this then, I started doing one thing after another to work with my fears by trying to conquer them. For example, I would go out on the street and beg for money, or I would go into stores and ask for food. To ask people for money or food was difficult for me because I saw myself as a well-bred, nice, responsible person who was very independent and would never ask anybody for anything. There was a lot of fear and intimidation around behaving in ways that challenged this self-image.

. . .

Then when I was twenty-five, I joined a spiritual group in San Francisco, where I was assigned a task I would have never undertaken on my own—to make up a song and sing it on Fisherman's Wharf. In the summertime on Fisherman's Wharf there are hundreds of tourists milling around, waiting to ride on the cable cars. My task was to sing for them. In other words, I was to purposefully make a fool of myself.

I was to sing the Bob Dylan-like song that I had made up in front of all those people, and then ask for money by holding out my derby hat. I had dressed up in a hippie outfit with a black derby hat, but not only was I not a hippie, I didn't even like hippies. And I certainly didn't want to be seen as one.

Even now I can remember standing there, petrified, trembling, thinking I was going to faint or throw up. But I was really motivated to get rid of my fear, so I sang my song and asked for money. Then a little while later, I did it again. Each time I did this it became easier. At one point, I realized I was even beginning to enjoy doing it. What I didn't realize is that I was just replacing one conditioned self with another. I had replaced this fearful self with one who was now confident in this situation.

Nor did I see that through this practice I was not really working with the roots of fear; I was working with the content of fear. When you're working with fear by trying to get rid of it, the content of fear can be infinite.

But at that point I didn't understand this. So, for the next few years, I practiced with fear by trying to get rid of it. At one point I decided I needed a job that would force me, on a daily basis, to go against the fearful patterns I wanted to eradicate. Although I had previously worked as a teacher and a computer programmer, I decided to get a job as a carpenter.

This was quite a leap into the unknown. For one thing, I weighed only 120 pounds, and more importantly, I had no physical skills. I was very aware that I would have to go out every day into a new situation that would threaten me and stretch my natural limits. This was my life for the next couple of years—daily facing my fears.

For example, once a group of us was sent out on a job to repair a beam high up in the ceiling of a factory. They put up the ladder—it must have been around thirty feet tall—and told me to go up and nail a support onto the beam. They didn't know I was afraid of heights, and I was afraid to tell them. As I climbed the ladder it seemed like it was shaking like Jell-O. When I got to the top and tried to nail in the support, my hands were shaking so badly I couldn't hit the nail. My supervisor yelled at me to come down, and I was so humiliated I couldn't even look at anybody.

There were many examples like this, where I felt humiliated. But I was very motivated to overcome my fears, so every morning I gave myself a pep talk so I'd be able to go to work and face whatever would come my way. Nonetheless, those first two years were very difficult.

Because the emotional agitation from fear is painful to experience, we have a natural aversion response. Who wants to reside with pain and discomfort? We try to escape it, overcome it, or smash through it.

At the same time, we often add a whole new negative aspect, experiencing anger and shame at ourselves for feeling afraid.

BUT HERE'S what I learned. What about seeing the fear as just another aspect of our conditioned mind? It's not that we're bad people because we have fear; due to our conditioning, fear is simply what is happening. And since this *is* what's happening, we could decide to really look at it by asking, "What *is* this experience?" This is essentially what the girl in Pema Chödrön's dream was doing.

The "what" of fear, as with all emotions, has two main components: thoughts and bodily sensations. Upon asking, "What is this experience?" we begin to hear the fear-based thoughts that scream through our minds: "I can't do this," "What's going to happen to me?", "This isn't how it's supposed to be," "Please stop."

We hear also the voices of self-condemnation: "I'll never be good enough," "I'm hopeless," and so on.

Can we learn to see these thoughts as just thoughts, even though they seem so solid?

Then we drop into the bodily experience of fear, with all its unpleasant sensations: agitation in the stomach and chest, narrowing of perceptions, tightness in the shoulders, rigidity in the mouth, queasiness, weakness.

By allowing ourselves to *be* afraid, we come to realize that this horrible feeling of dread is just a combination of some strong physical sensations and some deeply held beliefs about ourselves. The problem is not so much these sensations and thoughts, but our resistance to feeling them. Our desire to avoid fear, our negative attachment to it, is what makes us feel so horrible.

When we are willing to let the fear in, relating to it as a "what" instead of as "me," it loses its juice. We see that even though we may feel terror, there is no real physical danger. Instead of fighting fear with panic, or pushing it away, we let it in. We give up our fear of fear.

COURAGE IS NOT the absence of fear; courage is and grows out of the willingness to experience fear.

Cultivating the willingness to be with fear is a big step toward learning the willingness to be with our life as it is.

The experience of residing in fear is never a clear-cut progression. For me, during intense periods of fear, it was a moment-by-moment struggle. One moment I would want to run away, to push away the fear; the next moment I would want to smash through it.

There would also be moments of surrender, when I could say "Yes" to it and almost embrace it. Finally, I began to see that fear is not solid; that it is nothing more than strong sensations and disabling thoughts based on our conditioning.

For example, those who have stage fright, including the anxiety of public speaking, may feel the constant underground dread of having to deal with it. Fear of public speaking triggers the dread and shame of public failure and humiliation.

But what is really being threatened? Isn't it just our desired self-image of appearing strong, calm, insightful, or whatever our own particular narrow view is of who we're *supposed* to be? We certainly fear appearing weak or not on top of it. Why? Because that would confirm our own negative core beliefs of unworthiness.

Even though there is no real danger, isn't it true that the fear of failing often *feels* fatal? Yet ironically, our very attempt to fight the fear is most often what increases it, and may even result in panic.

There is a better alternative: as with the other basic fears, to effectively work with the fear of unworthiness we must learn to let it in willingly, to breathe the sensations of fear directly into the center of the chest. In other words, to say Yes to the fear.

At one point in my life, when I was struggling with my fear of giving public talks, I joined Toastmasters, a group designed to help develop skills in public speaking. But I didn't join to learn to give better talks, or even with the goal of overcoming my fear. I joined so that I could have a laboratory, a place to invite the fear in and go to its roots.

In a way, I actually began to look forward to the fear arising, so I could breathe it right into the heart, entering into it fully. Paradoxically, the willingness to be with the fear *completely* is what changes the experience of fear altogether. It's not that fear will no longer arise; it's that we no longer fear it.

EVENTUALLY, we all need to be willing to face the deepest, darkest beliefs we have about ourselves. Only in this way can we come to *know* that they are only *beliefs,* and not the truth about who we are.

By willingly entering into this process, by seeing through the fiction of who we believe ourselves to be, we can connect with our true nature.

As Nietzsche put it, "One must have chaos in oneself to give birth to a dancing star." Love is the dancing star, the fruit of saying Yes, of consciously and willingly facing our fears.

When we are willing to let fear in, we discover that we can have fear but not actually be afraid. When fear arises, instead of "Oh no!" we learn to say, "Here it comes again—what will it be like this time?" And what happens? The solidity and power of our fear gradually dissipates.

When we can willingly stay with our experience of fear without suppressing it, expressing it, wallowing in it, or judging it, our awareness becomes a wider container. Within that still container fear's thoughts and sensations can move through us.

As we become familiar with our fear, compassion naturally arises, lightening the whole struggle. It is here that we bring a sense of heart into our otherwise gloomy work with fear. At this point we might even experience a deep and pervasive peace, feeling the sense of spaciousness that arises as fear transforms.

Even now, my own practice path with fear continues. For the most part, I no longer live from the lifelong tunnel of fear that was running me. That tunnel seemed so real for so long, I don't think I ever really believed I could be free from it.

When fear arises for me now, although my mind may still desire for it to go away, there is also an almost instant recognition of what is going on. I then breathe into the center of my chest, inviting the fear in with a willingness to feel its texture.

But at the same time, I know that it is not all of who I am; it is just a part of me. My heart could be pounding and my stomach feeling queasy, which are simply the conditioned responses to perceived danger. But there is also lightness, a spaciousness, through which the conditioning of fear can be experienced.

WITH AWARENESS, the solidity of fear becomes porous. And what remains? Simply life itself, with an increasingly vaster sense of Being.

21

DEALING WITH PHYSICAL PAIN

Whether the pain is short term, like an injury, or long term, as with chronic pain, in the pain syndrome, our physical pain and our emotional reactions to it can become the primary focus of our attention. When this happens, our life begins to narrow down to revolve almost completely around how we're feeling.

With chronic pain we may not know how long the pain will last, and when or if it will go away; and if it goes, we don't know if it will return. We can become constantly anxious that the pain will never stop, and when it stops, even though we may be glad that we are no longer in pain, we can become anxious in anticipating that it will begin again.

What is happening is that our focus and personality begin to center more and more on our pain and its vicissitudes.

. . .

THE UNDERSTANDING that pain can be our path to self-realization is a fundamental change in how we relate to our experience; it allows us to begin to view and work with our pain, as well as our suffering, in a more conscious way.

At the very least, we can view our pain as an opportunity to learn from our many attachments—especially from our attachment to comfort. There is also attachment to our body and to control.

And in cases of chronic pain, there is also attachment to our future—the fear of what's going to happen to us. Yet, practicing with our pain is what allows us to gradually become free of these attachments, or at least to hold them more lightly.

Once we remember to relate to our pain more consciously, the one essential thing to recognize is that pain is one thing and how we relate to it is another. Often they get intermingled into one confused whole, rather than realizing that pain is the physical experience of discomfort and how we relate to it is more mental and emotional.

We may tend to relate to pain from the emotion of fear or self-pity, and this makes the experience of pain more intense. The alternative is to begin to relate to pain with an element of curiosity—being willing to relax into it and explore it—where the experience of pain is usually more tolerable.

~

NO MATTER how well we learn to deal with our pain, it's essential to understand that setbacks will most likely happen. When we understand this, we are less likely to be blindsided by them, and thus less likely to fall into a tailspin of discouragement and anxiety.

"*Setbacks will happen!*" is a mantra that anyone with chronic pain should commit to memory. Now, no longer surprised with each new episode, I have learned to remember to pause, take a breath into the heart, say "Hello" to the pain, and then greet it with curiosity.

As an antidote to focusing solely on our pain, we have to remember to at least occasionally shift our attention to the more positive things in our life. I even made a list of the things I most love to do, which I refer to when in pain, since it's so easy, when in pain, or depression or disheartenment, to forget about the things that can bring us joy. Sometimes finding distractions is the best thing we can do.

We also need to be aware of the tendency to isolate when we're in pain. We may isolate because we think that others can't possibly understand what we're going through, or we don't want to burden them. We may even feel guilty.

But these thoughts, along with feeling isolated and cut off from friends, just make our experience of pain more intense. One thing I've found is that, despite whatever hesitancy I had, it has always been helpful to talk to a friend—to honestly share what I am thinking and feeling. This isn't about looking for advice or expecting the other person to take away my pain; it's a reminder never to underestimate the value of genuine human connection.

Part of the wisdom that may be revealed as we work with our pain is understanding the paradox that, although we are basically alone, we are at the same time truly connected.

ANOTHER PERNICIOUS AND very common tendency of the thinking mind is catastrophizing—where we automatically exaggerate and magnify the threat of pain and anticipate the worst.

When we get trapped in this way of thinking, the whole experience can seem overwhelming. This is where we can tell ourselves, "Not happening now!"—a helpful reminder that we don't actually have a medical diagnosis right now. Or, even if we have a diagnosis, imagining the worst future scenarios just makes things much worse.

Using this phrase allows us to uncover how much mental spinning we're adding, and how it obscures the reality of the present moment. This phrase—"Not happening now"—is a reminder that most of what is causing us anxiety in the present moment is only happening in our mind.

DEEP RELAXATION BREATHING is another excellent way to lessen the severity of pain, and also lessen the panic that often accompanies our pain. Deep relaxation is based on a breathing technique that can trigger the body's natural ability to calm down. Here is a little background: The autonomic nervous system is divided into two branches —the sympathetic and the parasympathetic.

The sympathetic branch is associated with high levels of anxiety, rapid heartbeat, shakiness, panic, and other such things. The parasympathetic branch is associated with calm and a lower heart rate. *The two branches cannot dominate at the same time*, so the practice is to cultivate the parasympathetic response of calm and learn to be able to activate it and override the sympathetic response of panic.

With some practice, when you take slow, steady breaths, your brain gets the message that all is well and activates the parasympathetic response, which slows the heart rate and digestion and promotes feelings of calm. The parasympathetic response, by relaxing the body, also reduces the intensity of our pain.

Deep relaxation breaths entail breathing slowly and deeply through the nose and exhaling quietly and slowly through the slightly open mouth, as if breathing through a straw. The main focus is on breathing more slowly and more deeply than normal, without forcing it. It can help to keep time by shooting for roughly four seconds for each inhale and each exhale.

If it feels uncomfortable to breathe that slowly, it's okay to start to breathe at whatever rate feels more relaxed. But remember, it's the slower deeper breathing that triggers the parasympathetic nervous system response of calm and the ability to relax. When the body is relaxed, our pain automatically lessens.

~

ANOTHER EFFECTIVE WAY TO work with pain is to intentionally focus on the breath itself. Normally, when we're in pain, the painful sensations fill up the entire awareness channel connected to the brain.

Picture a conduit that sends the pain signals to the brain, and picture the conduit completely filled with the painful signals. But when we include a focused attention to the breath—which may require our full concentration—the pain only fills up part of the awareness channel, since awareness is so attuned to the breath.

This allows the pain to be experienced differently, within a larger container of awareness. Focusing on the breath is even more effective when we take the longer and slower breaths associated with deep relaxation. As the body relaxes, the intensity of physical pain will often lessen.

Additionally, an expanded version of focusing on the breath is to ask, "And?" This reminds us to ask where else we can direct our awareness, other than obsessively fixating on the pain. We can look to some other aspect of the present moment, such as sounds, or the air, or the temperature, or the sense of space. Bringing awareness to the environment will take our focus off of our pain and the pain will often feel less intense.

ONE OTHER EFFECTIVE way of working with the physical experience of pain itself is to focus on the specific physical sensations of the pain directly. We can do this by using the breath to breathe into the pain, bringing to it a sense of kindness. We breathe into the physical sensations almost as if the breath were giving a gentle massage to the pain.

I sometimes have periods of nausea, a symptom of the immune system disorder I've had for many years. When the nausea is intense, I often have to curl up into a fetal position in bed, and my practice is to breathe into the center of the chest on the in-breath and then extend kindness or healing energy to my body, to my immune system, via the out-breath—just as you would extend compassion to someone you cared about who was in distress.

When I touch into the nausea, I wordlessly say "Hello" to it, and remind it that it's not the enemy. With the increasing sense of spaciousness and heart that comes from practicing in this way, I have found I can gradually stay with the sensations of nausea for quite some time. And in the moments when I could experience the nausea not as "pain," but as just intense physical sensations, I'm sometimes struck by a sense of quiet joy, where it is clear that who we truly are is so much more than just this body.

~

REGARDLESS OF WHAT we might be feeling physically or emotionally, we can understand that we are not limited or defined by those feelings. Sometimes we can remember to say "Yes" to the pain, which means, instead of saying "No, not again," or "I can't stand this," we're willing to actually feel what's there.

Sometimes I even say, "Do your worst, pain!" This is not said with grim determination or as an angry defiance; it is actually a lighthearted attitude that helps me to avoid falling into feeling like a victim. It's no longer fighting what feels like the enemy; rather, it's a back-and-forth engagement that feels more poignant than like a struggle. In fact, sometimes it even feels a little playful.

~

ONE OTHER FORM of learning that comes from practicing with our pain is the increased awareness of other people who also may be suffering. Pain is the great equalizer—it humbles us into the realization that we're all in this life together.

In this way, our personal pain connects us with the pain of others—the pain we all share in various forms. This can deepen our sense of compassion and the wish that the suffering of others be healed. It will also diminish the sense of isolation we often feel when we're in pain.

When discouraged or feeling isolated, we can deepen our compassion further by actually doing something—even a little thing—to give ourselves to another. We can call up someone we know who is hurting. Or we can make ourselves available to someone even if we're not feeling well.

Along with whatever help we might be extending, this also takes our attention off of ourselves, which in itself can bring some relief. Helping others, even in little ways, also is one of the most effective ways of experiencing our basic connectedness, and is almost always satisfying.

22

PAIN AND SUFFERING

Pain and suffering are guaranteed to be part of the human experience. Jean-Dominique Bauby, the former editor-in-chief of the French magazine *Elle,* wrote a book called *The Diving Bell and the Butterfly*. This man had lived a very active and creative life, until one day in 1995, when he was only forty-three years old, he experienced a massive stroke that resulted in a rare condition called locked-in syndrome.

While his whole body was totally paralyzed, his mind was completely functional. After lying in bed for months, he discovered he could still flutter his left eyelid. With this discovery, he devised a form of communication, whereby the number of movements of this one eyelid would signify the different letters of the alphabet. This is how he spelled out each word, each sentence, of his book, poignantly chronicling his thoughts and feelings as he lay locked in his body. He died two days after his book was published.

In the one-page chapter called "My Lucky Day," the author describes how the alarm clock connected to his feeding tubes was ringing continuously for half an hour. The intensely piercing "beep, beep, beep" sound jackhammered into his brain. As he began sweating profusely, the sweat unglued the tape over his right eye, loosening his eyelashes to scratch his pupil. Then his urinary catheter fell out, leaving him soaked in his own urine. There he was, lying in bed with the piercing sounds, the irritated eye, and the drenched bed. At that moment a nurse came in, and oblivious to him, switched on the television. What he saw on the screen were the bold letters of a commercial asking, "Were you born lucky?"

The author relates this story without a trace of self-pity. It's primarily a description of his thoughts and sensations. To really appreciate the story, all we have to do is imagine ourselves in the same situation. What would our reactions be?

IN GENERAL, we don't want to have very much to do with pain. Most living creatures share this aversion. It appears to be a natural and even intelligent part of the evolutionary process. Yet, human beings seem unique in their ability to contort from their pain the state that we commonly call suffering.

The process starts with our natural tendency to avoid pain. Again, this is a fact of life: we don't like pain. But we suffer because we add our deep-seated belief that life *should* be free from pain to the experience of pain itself, thereby making the pain feel even worse.

In resisting our pain by holding to this belief, we strengthen just what we're trying to avoid. When we make pain the enemy, we solidify it. This resistance is where our suffering begins.

Again, on experiencing pain, we almost always immediately resist. On top of the physical discomfort, we quickly add a layer of negative judgments: "Why is this happening to me?", "I can't bear this," and so on. Whether or not we actually voice these judgments, we thoroughly believe them, which reinforces their devastating power.

Rather than see them as something that we add on, we accept them, unquestioned, as the truth. This blind belief in our thoughts further solidifies our physical experience of pain into the dense heaviness of suffering.

IN EARLY 1991, I had an acute and prolonged relapse of an immune system disease in which my muscles attack themselves. The main physical symptoms were intense muscle weakness, painful flu-like feelings—as if my cells were polluted—and worst of all, pervasive and relentless nausea.

Within two weeks, these physical symptoms had been supplemented by classical psychological symptoms: anger, self-pity, depression, and helplessness. I also felt hopelessness—the fear of being forever shut off from life.

I didn't want to complain, but I also felt isolated because I didn't know how to communicate what I was feeling. I felt guilt, because I couldn't fulfill my duties. I also felt a sense of shame, in the misguided belief that the illness proved that I was weak.

On the one hand, I had definitive and objective physical symptoms with which to deal. On the other, I had layer upon layer of dark emotion-based thoughts. These strongly believed thoughts exacerbated the physical symptoms into the experience of suffering, which has its own painful quality.

At first it was not an option to go directly into my pain. I certainly couldn't encounter my nausea head-on. But gradually approaching the pain from the edges made a more direct approach possible.

No longer believing the thoughts, no longer fighting the resistance, left me with just the physical sensations of nausea. But now it was a physical experience without the suffering!

I saw clearly how we hold our suffering in place with fear-based thoughts that arise in reaction to pain. These thoughts are further solidified by our resistance to letting the pain just be.

As often as I was able, I would breathe into the center of the chest on the in-breath, and then extend loving kindness to my body, to my immune system, via the out-breath. With this sense of spaciousness and heart, I found that I could enter directly into the sensations of nausea, where it no longer felt uncomfortable.

OPENING to pain in itself may still not be possible if the pain is intense, but in many cases, pain is not as unbearable as we *think* it is. Although the sensations may remain unpleasant, it is often possible for us to actually experience them.

Working with our pain and suffering requires both the precision of seeing clearly through our believed thoughts and a softening awareness that allows us to enter with a light touch into those areas we have tended to avoid. Working in this way, we see how much of our suffering is unnecessary.

This clarity in turn gives us the courage to continue working with suffering, even in those moments when it seems like it will never end. What arises is an increasing compassion for both ourselves and the whole human drama. We see that pain and suffering are not the endgame; they are simply the most effective vehicles for awakening our hearts.

Years later, in reflecting on these events, I thought of Thomas Merton's words, "True love and prayer are learned in the moment when prayer has become impossible and the heart has turned to stone."

HISTORY, among other things, is the history of pain and suffering and death. Seventy-five million people died during the Black Plague in the fourteenth century; fifty million died in the 1918 influenza pandemic; sixty million people died in World War II. How many will eventually die from the coronavirus?

The coronavirus, the pandemic flu from a century ago, and the Black Plague in Europe are merely concentrated and dramatic instances of a perpetual truth: that all of us are vulnerable to meeting our death at any time —by a virus, an accident, or any number of seemingly random causes.

We speak of underlying conditions, but in a sense, simply being alive is an inescapable "underlying condition."

The awareness that everyone who has ever lived has died or will die is a necessary insight to be internalized. But not in a morbid way; rather, as an aid to living with clarity and awareness. From the moment we are born, the one thing that is meant to happen is that we will die. The only questions are when, where, and how.

How do we internalize the fact that our own death is certain? And how do we balance this insight with the equally important understanding that, in the big scheme of things, our death is of no consequence?

Once we can understand the magnitude of our existential condition—that being alive almost guarantees that, at some point, we will experience pain—we can pay more attention to the human tendency to turn our pain into suffering. As we bring precision to seeing clearly through the believed thoughts that guarantee our suffering, we can gradually become free of it. Some pain may remain, but without the suffering that we put on top of it, we can experience a sense of freedom and equanimity that we may never have thought possible.

"THE WORLD BREAKS everyone and afterward many are strong at the broken places."—Ernest Hemingway

23

DISTRESS AND WORK

We may have the good fortune to have long periods between episodes of distress and suffering. But there may still be many moments where we experience life as difficult. This is particularly true in our work.

When contemplating what our life work might be, our attachment to security and a sense of safety is what usually drives us. We act out of the unconscious belief that we can avoid experiencing the sense of groundlessness inherent in change and uncertainty.

WHEN I WAS in my twenties, working first as a teacher and then as a computer programmer, I lived every day with a pervasive sense of anxiety, based in a vague dissatisfaction with what I was doing. But even though I knew that my work would never bring me genuine satisfaction, I didn't know what to do. I told my closest friend about my problem, and he suggested I stop thinking about it, and instead, whenever the issue arose in my mind, that I simply stay present with the anxiety and confusion that would accompany my indecision.

His advice made no sense to me at the time, but I was desperate, so I followed his instructions as best I could. Weeks went by with no clarity, and then one day, when I was helping some friends with a physical task, I was struck with lightning-bolt clarity that I should become a carpenter.

It made no logical sense. I had no skills and weighed only 120 pounds, but as the philosopher Pascal once said, "The heart has reasons of which the mind knows nothing."

What I learned from that experience, and with subsequent similar experiences, is that difficult decisions, like what life path to follow, are not made through thinking and analysis but from the heart.

Yet following through on decisions like these might require entering into unknown territory, where the primary emotional feeling is one of groundlessness. But ironically, entering into groundlessness itself is the key to resolving our problem. Our willingness to experience the physical sense of no ground is what will eventually bring us to clarity, because it will allow us to see through the roots of our fears.

This is not to say that we throw all of our thinking aside. There will always be practical considerations—money, education, and so on—but these logistical factors cannot be our main focus in settling on what our work will be.

PERHAPS THE ONE factor that is not given enough focus is the question, "What do I have to offer?"

The way we approach our work life is often deeply rooted in our upbringing. Beginning when I was eleven, I worked for my father during the summer for ten years. My brother and sisters and I were the sales force for his souvenir store on the boardwalk in Atlantic City. Although we were pretty aggressive salespeople, when my father perceived that business was not going well, he would sometimes explode in anger. Unfortunately, the anger was usually directed at one of his children; most often, it seemed, at me. He was quite powerful when he was angry. He would shout about how I wasn't trying, how I was unappreciative, how I was just going through the motions.

When he'd shout like this, everyone in the store would freeze. Then, when he stomped out of the store, the nervous customers, especially the customers I was waiting on, would start buying like crazy. Looking back, this seems almost comical, but at the time good humor was far from my mind.

As angry as I'd get when I felt I'd been unjustifiably picked on, I was nonetheless your typical good boy and would proceed to try harder. At one point, I started listing all my sales and adding them up at the end of the day. I'd show this list to my father to prove to him that I was measuring up.

For many years, in a variety of contexts, I continued this strategy of "making a list" to prove that I was worthy. I felt that if I could tangibly demonstrate my success, my productivity, my value, it would ward off the core fear of being judged as unworthy.

Of course, this strategy, like all strategies of behavior modification, never really worked. Perhaps it allowed me to achieve external success in that it drove me to excel, but it never addressed the core fear. The core fear, and all of the day-to-day anxiety that arose out of it, could only be put at bay temporarily.

As long as we don't see clearly that we are just acting from pictures of how we *should* be, and as long as we don't open up to experiencing the layers of protection and fear that underlie most of these pictures, any meaningful transformation will elude us.

When I finally started seeing this dynamic for what it was, I was able to approach my deeply ingrained behavior pattern quite differently. Instead of trying to live out of the picture that I had to measure up, instead of following the behaviors of "making my lists," I learned to bring awareness to the fear itself.

EACH OF US has to see our own version of "making a list." Is your style to get hooked into the "child" identity, needing to please and get approval from someone whom you blindly identify as an authority? Or perhaps you have a pattern of defiance to prove your worth.

Or is your pattern to be busy, busy, busy, with the anxious feeling that you're trying to juggle at least one too many plates? Can you see the addictive quality of the busyness, how you use it to validate your own worth, to distract yourself from the underlying fear of being "nothing"?

Although we believe that we *have* to do all of the things on our plate, all it takes is a prolonged bout of illness to see that this is not true. We are not indispensable, and much of what we think we have to do can be delegated, put on hold, or even deleted.

The problem is not how much work we have to do, but how we're using that work to bolster and solidify our identity. Living the life of self-discovery is about becoming free of any restricting identity, especially those based primarily in fear. In other words, sooner or later we will have to deal with the groundlessness that comes when our false sense of security is challenged or removed.

Sooner or later, we'll have to go to the roots of the fears and beliefs that tell us, in one way or another, that we're not and never will be quite good enough. This is a crucial part of the path of self-realization and inner freedom.

24

RELATIONSHIPS

"What is hell? Hell is the suffering of being unable to love," wrote Dostoevsky in *The Brothers Karamazov*. Indeed, we may have knowledge and deep insight, we may practice awareness and be mindful, but without kindness and love, something essential will always be lacking.

Until we can truly surrender to love, our aspiration to live most genuinely will not be fulfilled.

Yet, isn't it true that we rarely experience this sort of love? Isn't it much more common to experience relationships as a source of difficulty? This is not only true with relationships with our mates, but also with our parents, our children, our bosses, and even our friends.

So why is there so much difficulty? Or, more pointedly, what is it that each of *us* brings to relationships that seems to cause so many problems?

The answer is: ourselves! We bring our assumptions, our hopes, and most of all, our wants. Whenever we want something from someone, which is always true when we have expectations and requirements of them, we can't really see them as people. We only see them in terms of what we want them to provide. And as long as we want something from them, our capacity for love is blocked.

When we think we love a person, often it is not the actual person that we relate to but our image of who the person is, and we may never see the person for who they really are.

This might lead to difficulties around intimacy or trust; around fears of criticism or rejection; or around feeling unappreciated or controlled. Certainly, money issues and sexual issues can cause us difficulties. And it's this very fact, that relationships often trigger our most painful and unhealed emotions, that makes them such a potentially useful teacher.

WE OFTEN WANT other people to *be* a certain way, primarily so that *we'll* feel a certain way, such as safe, confident, loved, pleasured, happy, appreciated, etc. For example, when we believe someone loves us and wants us, we not only feel loved but also *worthy* of love, which is often the balm we crave to cover over our basic fears of unworthiness.

But if our needs and expectations are not met in that relationship, we often feel unloved, rejected, lonely, and unappreciated. Again, think of your own situation to see how this specifically applies. *We need to see that almost all of our relationship difficulties come from our wanting someone or something to be different.*

We often forget that these difficulties present the most valuable opportunities to learn about ourselves, especially our *own* barriers. In relationships, the other person is, in fact, a mirror reflecting back to us *exactly* what needs clarifying—our expectations, our judgments, our anger, and our fear.

Think of a difficult relationship. Can you see how you're often unwilling to give, primarily because you're not getting what you want, and how quickly a power struggle ensues before you're even aware of its roots?

In relationships, particularly when we have an emotional reaction, we'll almost always focus on the *other* person instead of looking inward. What we're really trying to do is change that person so they'll fulfill our hopes and expectations.

> We *wish for people to accept us as we are,* but in so doing *we reject them for who they are.*

Again, almost all of our difficulties in relationships come from wanting people to be different than they are. The point is: we block the possibility of real connection with people when we require that they be different.

In these power struggles, we may even view the other person as our enemy, leading us to either erect barriers of protection or attack in order to defend ourselves. We must be honest about this.

But can you see how fear is a key issue underlying most of our relationship difficulties? Fear, more than anything, is what blocks intimacy and love.

These fears are not necessarily logical or reasonable. For example, fearing that we're unworthy of love doesn't mean it's true. It just means that we *believe* it to be true; consequently, so long as we remain caught in our belief, that fear will control the way we act, react, and relate to others.

Yet, when we reveal our fears, something changes. For example, when we reveal our fear of loneliness, without trying to embellish it, it loses its solidity. As Nietzsche pointed out, it is a paradox—that isolation exists only in isolation; once shared, it melts away.

The task itself is very straightforward, yet it is nonetheless very difficult to do: we need to refrain from replaying our story line of drama and blame and instead say Yes to the present moment of our experience—to actually *feel* it, to rest in the bodily sensations no matter how uncomfortable they may be.

We might think we can't stand it, but of course we can. We just don't want to. We believe we can't be happy because our life is difficult. This is backwards. We can't be truly happy *until* our life is difficult.

UNTIL WE FACE OUR FEARS, we will not be able to truly connect with others, because we'll still be disconnected from ourselves. If we don't become intimate with our own fears, how can we have a healthy relationship with another who is also caught in fear?

But as we learn to befriend our fears, we no longer fear them; and when we meet someone who may be angry at us, instead of immediately reacting to the anger, we may understand that they're really just afraid.

The path to awakening the heart of compassion toward another is always rooted in our acceptance of our own pain.

This is particularly true when we realize that the most difficult thing for us to give to another is often what the other wants most. For example, in giving nonjudgment to another, which is what everyone wants and also one of the hardest things to give, we're actually giving *ourselves* a great gift.

This gift is the opportunity to see that *our judgments*

and criticisms are always more about us than they are about the other person. This understanding gives us the matrix to work more easily and directly with our deepest fears and attachments.

It is well known that humans tend to have a confirmation bias: once we have decided someone is a bad person, we start looking for evidence to support our assumption, based on that existing bias. However, if we can recognize this and instead try to find evidence that we may be wrong, this can make a huge difference in our relationships. This doesn't mean accepting inappropriate behavior, but simply trying to see the good in people, even if we don't agree with them in every way.

No one is perfect, and our connections deepen when we honor one another's imperfections.

ONE PRACTICE that is particularly helpful in working with our judgments and criticisms of another is called "Just Like Me." When we become aware of our judgments, if we say "just like me," we can immediately look inward and see that we are not essentially different from the other person.

Even if we don't manifest exactly like the other, we can at least see our own similar inclinations and patterns, which automatically lighten our tendency toward self-righteousness and even indignation.

The point is, when we no longer relate primarily from our self-centered motivation to have life be the way we want it to be, our relationships can become one of the most fruitful paths to the depth of happiness that we're all looking for.

We can discover the simple but profound truth that *love is not about having someone else make us happy; love is about wanting them to be happy.*

When we love another, it is defined by wanting to do for the other. And as James Keller said, "A candle loses nothing by lighting another candle."

Søren Kierkegaard, the nineteenth-century Christian existentialist, said that perfect love is to love the one through whom one became unhappy. To put it another way, the more we work with our own unhappy reactions, the more the path is cleared for love to simply flow through us. The more we remove the conditions we impose on our relationships, the more open the way to unconditioned love.

We don't have to open our hearts. The heart is already open. We just need to clear the obstructions that get in the way of experiencing that openness.

Working with our own reactions takes a particularly interesting twist because, as stated earlier, what we want most from another is often what is most difficult for them to give. The converse is also true: what's most difficult for us to give is often what another wants most.

This twist shines light on exactly what Kierkegaard meant by perfect love being the love that comes from our unhappiness. If we see where we're stuck in not wanting to give to another what the other wants, and if we're willing to work with the layers of anger and fear within that place, then it becomes the path to freedom.

To counteract fear-based withholding might require intentional acts of generosity, not in order to be virtuous, but to push ourselves to the edge in order to face our fears. The more honestly and clearly we see and experience our fears, the less they will dictate our behavior.

As we give—and work with what gets in the way of giving—we heal. Generosity gradually becomes our natural inclination. Healing ourselves in this way indirectly also heals the other because it gives them the option of slowly lowering their own protective barriers. This differs from trying to change the other, from getting them to give us what we want. Practice is about working on ourselves only, on our own unhappiness. Yet each effort to bring spaciousness around our own fears allows spaciousness to arise around the other's fears as well.

When Elizabeth and I came together as a couple, I was struggling with my tendency to be critical and judgmental. I'd seen the harm that this tendency had done in the past, and I was clear that I needed to work with it. It was also clear that Elizabeth was not the least bit interested in being fixed.

I made it my practice to avoid criticizing her as much as possible. At first it was difficult, because what is an ego if not a collection of opinions, identities, and behaviors—all of which we believe? When a judgment about another person crosses our mental screen, we normally simply accept it as the truth, and it's hard to keep our mouth shut.

In making the effort to not express my critical judgments, I learned something amazing. My judgments were never about her; they were always about me! The perfect example of this lies in our different styles regarding possessions. I like owning very little. Elizabeth, on the other hand, enjoys finding thrift-store treasures. It's not that she's materialistic; it's just that her joy comes from bringing home a load from the Goodwill, whereas my joy comes from being able to throw something out. What I do own, I like to keep neat and orderly. Elizabeth, on the other hand, likes having it all out there where she can see it.

It may seem that my style—being simple, neat, and orderly—is saner and Zen-like. Before I met Elizabeth, I certainly believed this to be true. But when I started practicing withholding my critical judgments, I began to see things quite differently. When I'd see Elizabeth's style, instead of telling her how much better it would be for her if she were more orderly, I began to pay attention to the emotional state from which my judgments were arising. Had I simply expressed my judgments, I would never even have seen my own inner state. And what did I see? I saw fear. I saw my own fear of chaos. My tendency toward orderliness and neatness was not some Zen virtue so much as a strategy of control—a way of avoiding my fear of chaos, as well as the feeling of helplessness at the loss of control.

Seeing this clearly made it easy to avoid expressing my judgments to Elizabeth. I understood that what I needed to do was tend to my own discomfort. Ordinarily we simply assume it's the other person's job to take our discomfort away. But on the path of self-discovery, nothing could be farther from the truth. Our discomfort is *our* job.

What's so interesting about human dynamics is that once we attend to our job—seeing our beliefs and experiencing the fears from which they arise—it usually frees the other to move toward us. When the other no longer feels the need to defend, within that spaciousness they, too, become more willing to attend to *their* job.

. . .

We don't have to *try* to feel loving or kind; we just have to work with what gets in the way, particularly where we hold our hearts back in fear.

This brings us closer to fulfilling our life task: to know the truth of who we really are—that the nature of our Being is connectedness and Love.

Our task is not to change others to suit us, but to know the world through Love.

As we begin to know the world through Love, our actions in the world come more and more naturally from a true understanding of who we are. And when situations arise where we don't know what to do or say, we can ask the pivotal practice question: "*What would it mean, in this very moment, to live from kindness?*"

As we breathe into the center of the chest, we allow the answer to come not from the mind but from the heart. It is at this point that our personal love begins to merge with the bigger love that is our true nature.

Sometimes when I look at Elizabeth and see her kind heart and deep aspiration, I naturally step through the portal into Big Love. The love is then directed toward all equally, the same way the sun shines on everything without discrimination.

Genuine kindness is devoid of judgment; it excludes no one. It embraces all and everything. Love gives without the expectation that it will get something in return.

> *Love gives with no agenda, with no purpose.*
> *Love, on this level, simply* is.
> *It is the natural state of our unobstructed*
> *Being.*

25

SEX

A young meditation student realized he had some sexual difficulties. He thought about going to his teacher for help, but felt a lot of hesitation: "Maybe it's not appropriate to talk to my teacher about sex. What's he going to think of me?" He went to the teacher anyway, and described the situation. The teacher told him, "We must struggle with desire. We must *struggle* with desire. Go back to your meditation cushion, and learn what it means to struggle with desire."

The dutiful and persevering student went back to his cushion and struggled and struggled with his desire. But for some reason he didn't get very far. In fact, it seemed like his problem became even worse. So, he decided to go to another teacher.

This time he went to a teacher who was very famous for his deep wisdom. He told the teacher about his situation. The teacher peered at him in an inscrutable way, and said, "No sex. No *not* sex. Not one. Not two." And he rang his bell, dismissing the student.

The student was impressed by this teaching, but

when he got back to his cushion, he had no idea what to do with it. Finally, he decided to go to another teacher, one famous for his ardent devotion to practice. The student went to the teacher and described his problem.

The teacher said, "Okay, this is what you need to do. Whenever your sexual difficulty arises in your mind, you just stop whatever you're doing and do 108 full bows, thinking only of your wish to live from compassion." The student really liked this advice, because now he had something he could do, something that he saw as being right in the heart of practice.

The student followed the third teacher's advice and became very, very good at bowing. But after some time, he felt as though he were squeezing a balloon right in the middle: as the middle would scrunch up, both ends were close to bursting at the seams. He realized he still wasn't addressing the situation.

Even though the student was discouraged, he decided to go to yet another teacher. He saw that maybe he was trying too hard, pushing too hard; so he decided to see a teacher who was famous for being laid back. He went to this teacher and described his situation. The teacher said, "No problem. Just be one with it. Just let it go."

By this time, the student was becoming cynical. He realized this advice was just words. But still, he had a real aspiration to deal with his situation. He didn't want to just shove it under the carpet.

Again, he found another teacher. And finally, in this last teacher's reply, he understood what all the other teachers were telling him: "We don't talk about sex here."

LIKE MOST OF the other "Zen stories" in this book, I made this up. Nevertheless, it can help us understand our own situation. It's true: we *don't* talk about sex, at least in terms of spiritual practice—and especially in public.

Why not? Because even though sexual themes, as well as so-called sexual freedom, are running through the mainstream of our culture, as a culture we still view sex with definitive moral overtones.

Regardless of whether we're conscious of this perspective, we still regard sexuality as something dark and forbidden. Even though we may not be conscious of this shadowy undercurrent, it's deeply embedded in our collective cellular memory.

As practitioners, the first thing we need to do is bring sexuality issues into the context of awareness. This is how we make them part of our practice world. We need to see our own expectations in this area. Because they may be hidden, they're often not what we think they are.

For example, we may have been raised in a family where sex was rarely talked about, or where there was little physical affection. Yet sexual freedom might have been very much the norm on television, in the movies, and among our friends. Although we speak the words of sexual freedom, and even act seemingly freely, underneath it all we may still experience sex in terms of guilt and shame, or at the very least, from a slightly prudish point of view.

What we have to look into is the beliefs and attitudes that we haven't questioned, the ones we still experience as the unexamined truth.

What do we require of our partner? Do we know what these requirements are? Do we expect that our partner should respond whenever we want them to—that their role is to satisfy us? Do we believe that too much sex is unreasonable? Or do we have the attitude that not enough sex is unreasonable? Do we have the view that if our partner is not satisfied in the sexual relationship, it means that somehow we're defective or deficient?

PRACTICING with so-called sexual problems often has little to do with sex itself, but instead with the overall patterns we've brought into the relationship. Often our impulses are the product of our minds rather than the natural arising of sexual energy.

Just look at our fantasies, our love for the forbidden, or the pernicious judging and evaluating of sexual performance. How often do we experience or appreciate sexuality apart from the filters of our thoughts and conditioning?

The main questions we need to raise are: To what extent are we driven by cultural morality, which often goes unseen? How much are we driven by thoughts, fears, and core beliefs?

The point is, in sex, as well as in all the other areas of our life, we need to be aware. Again, awareness is what heals.

This is certainly not to say that working with difficulties around sex will be easy. For example, it is natural as we get older for our sexual desires to gradually diminish. For many, especially men, this can feel as if our life is over, like our last vestige of youth is now gone.

AFTER I HAD surgery for kidney cancer, I had to be catheterized for several weeks, and for over two months having sex was out of the question. I had never even considered this before—I apparently had the unconscious belief that I would be able to continue having sex indefinitely. At first the thought of not having sex again was a big blow—like something essential to my being was possibly gone forever.

But as I breathed the acute feelings of loss into the chest center, something shifted in my understanding. I realized that far from my life now being a failure, I still had the possibility for genuine intimacy with Elizabeth, and perhaps on an even deeper level.

By acknowledging the possibility that we could no longer have the same kind of sexual relationship, and surrendering to the feelings of loss, I actually accepted it, and, to my great surprise, was truly okay with it. I also felt a sincere and heartfelt willingness to move toward a new kind of intimacy.

Happily for me my ability to have sex returned, but I learned something important, and gave up at least a little of my attachment to my body. With each loss we are given the opportunity to become free of our attachments. If we lose our ability to have sex or lose our partner, we may gradually become freer of our attachment to our sexual desires, and instead channel our attention to creative activities that we might not have previously undertaken, like writing, art, gardening, or whatever we might feel we formerly missed out on doing. Or we could channel our attention into new friendships, finding a different kind of connection than physical intimacy.

ALTHOUGH STRUGGLES with our sexuality can without doubt be difficult, it is also true that sometimes our most difficult experiences are the ones that enrich us the most. One key is perseverance—or simply not giving up. One of my favorite aphorisms, even if it's perhaps been overused, is still a great reminder: "Seven times down, eight times up."

26

THE DRY SPOT AND DEPRESSION

The very first time I sat in formal meditation, I had the distinct and eerie sensation that my body had disappeared. Though I'd never sat before, I'd received good instructions before the forty-minute sitting, and I tried very hard to stay focused. I can't say I didn't have expectations—I at least had the expectation that meditation would help me become calm. But I certainly didn't expect to feel that my body disappeared!

When I told the sitting instructor about it, he called what I'd experienced a "free ride." He said that many people sit for ten or twenty years hoping for just such an experience. I remember wondering why anyone would want to feel like that.

Later, I learned about free rides, those new and interesting states of mind that seem to come so easily in the beginning stages on the path of self-discovery. But when I was in the middle of this honeymoon stage—where everything seems so fresh and so mysterious—I simply took these exciting highs to be a natural part of the process.

As the honeymoon wore thin, however, as disappointment upon disappointment set in, as my projections and illusions became uncovered, I experienced periods of doubt.

Any honest practice will include periods of doubt. Questions will arise: "What am I really doing with my life?" And our experience of practice may become very dry.

The "dry spot" can be an acute, dramatic, and short-term condition, or a subtle, chronic, long-term process. In either case, when we hit the dry spot, not only is the honeymoon over, but we also have little connection with the aspiration that originally brought us to practice.

The dry spot is often the result of unfulfilled expectations about the path. It isn't bringing us the immediate peace, calm, or freedom from fear that we had hoped for. Disappointment often leads to anger, and anger leads to resistance.

When it becomes clear that neither the practice nor the teacher will save us, we blame the practice for being inadequate or the teacher for being flawed. Negative projections replace our pretty pictures. We lose touch with our aspiration, choosing instead to stew in our negative thoughts and opinions about practice.

It's important to understand that there's nothing wrong with the process of vacillating between aspiration and resistance. The dry spot is one particular and predictable manifestation of this natural cycle. But the first few times it hit me, it didn't seem natural at all. The perceptions that arose seemed like permanent truths about reality, rather than believed thoughts based on the changing cycles of a process.

This can be difficult, because the thoughts seem so true, so solid, so compelling. But as we stay with our experience, even as the anguish of not knowing remains, the dryness can be transfused with a deeper sense of aspiration.

Thomas Merton expressed this clearly: "True love and prayer are learned in the moment when prayer has become impossible and the heart has turned to stone."

THE EXPERIENCE of depression is one particularly difficult form of the dry spot, where our motivation to practice can become completely dormant. Added to the loss of motivation is the very common experience that we don't even know that we're depressed.

The trick is to try to view the depression with the curiosity of a scientist—as something to study objectively. In a way, this is a subtle version of seeing the depression as our path. The idea is that by studying the thoughts and feelings that constitute the depression, it will become increasingly less solid, thereby freeing us from its somber grip.

It can be a difficult step to see our depression as the path to awakening, because when depressed, we lack both the motivation and energy to do anything. This is why it is so important to learn to take one small step. Invoking curiosity can be that one small step.

To study the depression with curiosity, we start by objectively looking at what the mind is believing. Asking, *"What is my most believed thought?"* will no doubt turn up some versions of "I'm no good" or "What's the point?" or "Everything's hopeless." Just naming these thoughts takes away at least some of their power.

Then we ask the question *"What is this experience?"*—

bringing curiosity to what we're feeling in the body. Is it heaviness? Where do we feel it? What does the heaviness actually feel like? By entering into the body in this way, we are breaking our identification with the depression as being who we are.

AFTER I HAD surgery for kidney cancer, I had a series of co-morbidities that resulted in a heavy bout of depression. I hadn't experienced a sustained depression for many years, and, along with the physical symptoms, it seemed overwhelming.

When I asked myself what the most believed thought was, at first my mind was blank. It was like there were no thoughts. But I kept asking, and at one point it became crystal clear that my belief was "My life is over." Just seeing this clearly made the belief a little more porous.

Then I turned to feeling the experience in my body. Prior to this I felt basically numb, which is characteristic of depression. What I felt was an overwhelming sense of heaviness—a heaviness that was pressing down on me from above.

I actually became curious about what I was experiencing, and it gradually became clear, from staying with the experience, that it felt like I was pressing down feelings that I didn't want to feel.

Going deeper into my experience, it became obvious that what I was "depressing" were the feelings of fear and uncertainty—a fearful uncertainty about what my life would be if I didn't recover. Fortunately, this deep insight lifted the heaviness and allowed me to feel somewhat inwardly free.

. . .

HOWEVER, regardless of what we do, there may be times when the experience of depression feels too strong to stay with. When this occurs, we can take deep relaxing breaths, as in the deep breathing meditation—where we breathe in slowly through the nose and breathe out slowly through the slightly open mouth.

When the depression is really too strong to stay with in any way, we can consider medication. For lesser depression we can temporarily find distractions. For example, just taking walks outside—which we may initially resist doing—may help the depression lift.

This is how we come to the critical understanding that even while the emotion of depression might remain, we do not have to identify with it as being the truth, or who we are. This is what it means to be free from it; it's not that it's no longer present, but that it decreasingly dictates who we are or how we live.

THE REAL QUESTION IS THIS: Can our aspiration to live authentically become more important than indulging the stories of depression? Eventually, we all need to be willing to face the deepest, darkest beliefs we have about ourselves. Only in this way can we come to know that they are only beliefs—and not reality.

By willingly entering into this process, we can see through the fiction of who we believe ourselves to be. Love is the fruit of consciously and willingly facing our depression. Once consciously faced, it no longer blocks the love that is our true nature from coming forth freely on its own

We have to remember that the path of self-realization is about turning away from constantly seeking comfort and trying to avoid unpleasantness. Then we can turn away from our comfort-seeking behavior and resume our search to experience the truth of who we really are.

To think we should be superstars on the path of self-realization—immune to depression and fear—is just imagination, and it prevents us from simply slowing down and being present to whatever is on our plate. But slowing down and letting life just be is what allows us to get off the treadmill of depression and begin to do the things we love.

27

CONSCIOUS LIVING

Becoming more conscious or awake is not confined to periods of meditation or working with periods of difficulties, such as physical or emotional pain. Conscious living means being awake, as much as possible, throughout the entire day. The following practical suggestions are meant as guidelines to the experience of conscious living.

CONSCIOUS EATING

There are several books out on mindful eating, and they are no doubt valuable. However, I believe the following three basic suggestions for conscious eating would be an excellent start.

FIRST, REFLECT at the very beginning of the meal. Before eating, look at your food and be conscious of where it came from, and see if you can feel gratitude for having it. You could also use these few moments to remember people you know who are hurting and wish them well.

SECOND, PAUSE between each bite. Place your utensil down as you chew so as to refrain from speeding through the meal.

THIRD, EXPERIENCE the taste and texture of the food, and as you sit there, also experience the environment around you.

IF YOU DO these three things, your experience of eating will become not only more conscious, but also more enjoyable.

CONSCIOUS WALKING

I learned a form of conscious walking from the Vietnamese Zen teacher Thich Nhat Hanh in the early 1980s, and I've continued doing it for over forty years. It's called "gatha walking." The term *gatha* means "verse," and in gatha walking we silently repeat the verse as we walk, using it to direct our attention in specific ways.

Gatha walking was once described as the ambrosia of meditations, in part because it requires much less effort than most sitting meditations, but also because it is almost always delightful to do.

. . .

THE INSTRUCTIONS ARE FAIRLY SIMPLE: Wherever you are walking, at whatever pace, conscious walking encourages us to engage the senses—seeing, hearing, smelling, touching. To help avoid getting lost in daydreams, we silently repeat a verse, over and over. The gatha is usually very short and simple, but the words are meaningful, and help keep the focus on really being here.

THE VERSE that I've been using for some time has four lines:

When I walk the mind will wander.
With each sound the mind returns.
With each breath the heart is open.
With each step I touch this earth.

IT IS best to repeat the verse for the duration of the walk, even if you start feeling very open and spacious; otherwise, it's easy to become more spacey than spacious. As we walk, we bring awareness to the environment, using the lines to direct our attention. For example, the first line —"When I walk the mind will wander"—is a way of simply acknowledging the fact that our mind constantly wanders. There's no judgment that the mind's wandering is bad; it's just an objective acknowledgment.

WITH THE SECOND LINE—"WITH each sound the mind returns"—we direct attention to the sounds, to help bring us back to present-moment reality. I live close to the ocean, so I have the good fortune to regularly walk along the beach, where I not only use the sounds of the ocean and the gulls, but also the presence of wind, the feeling of the sun on my face, the smell of salt water, and whatever other sensory input arises.

Being in a beautiful place like the beach provides a very rich sensory world to take in and appreciate, but we don't have to be at the ocean or in the woods for conscious walking to be a rich experience; I have also had wonderful experiences gatha walking on the busy streets of New York City.

WITH THE THIRD LINE—"WITH each breath the heart is open"—we are not trying to maintain a disciplined focus on the breath. Rather, the breath is very lightly held as it is felt in the center of the chest. Sometimes, it feels as if the breeze goes right through me. With this line, as with the others, we stay with it for the duration of a few breaths before moving on to the next.

ON THE LAST LINE—"WITH each step I touch this earth"—we can feel the experience of literally walking on the earth, feeling appreciation for the preciousness of the opportunity to be alive. There is an unmistakable sense of presence, of *hereness*, that is the essence of living awake.

In conscious walking, we are not trying to feel a particular way, nor are we walking toward a particular destination; rather, each step is complete in itself. Each step is of ultimate value. At the same time, with each step, we are cultivating a much larger sense of what life is.

One beauty of conscious walking is that it can be done at any time, regardless of how long the walk is. We can just as easily do it walking to the mailbox as we can taking a walk in the woods.

CONSCIOUS TALKING

A lot has been said about communication skills, including many useful techniques. Also, I've found using the following three basic reminders is sufficient to cut through the complex world of human interaction.

Curiosity

Ask questions to draw out the other person, and try to listen with genuine interest. Focusing on oneself tends to dampen curiosity about another.

Attention

Pay complete attention to the person as they speak. Refrain from advising, defending, interrupting, or planning what to say next.

"We have two ears and one mouth so that we can listen twice as much as we speak." —Epictetus

Remember

If you are feeling judged or defensive or criticized, try to remember the following aphorism: *Everybody has pain. Everybody suffers. Everyone will someday die.*

Remembering these words makes it possible to step out of our reactions and see the other person in a new way.

. . .

CONSCIOUS SLEEPING

I have found one simple breathing practice that helps me at those times when I awaken in the middle of the night and can't go back to sleep.

DEEP RELAXATION BREATHING: On the in-breath, breathe slowly and deeply in through the nose, directing the attention and the breath into the center of the chest, and on the out-breath, breathe slowly and deeply through the very slightly open mouth. As much as possible let awareness reside in the heart, so that any agitation can settle down.

Even if I don't go back to sleep right away, I find the conscious awareness of the heart's breath is inherently satisfying, and I am content to simply reside in the breath and the heart.

CONSCIOUS MEDITATING

There are literally hundreds of different ways to meditate. The following meditation—called Head, Heart, Hara—which I do daily, is one proven way to cultivate both focus and energy.

IN THIS MEDITATION we bring attention to the head, the heart, and the hara.

In bringing attention to the head, we focus on the spot between the eyes, right above the bridge of the nose.

In bringing attention to the heart, we focus on the area right in the center of the chest, between the breasts.

Hara is the Japanese word for abdomen, and in

focusing on the hara, we bring attention to the spot approximately two inches below the navel.

WHY DO we focus on each of these three places?

Each of the places—the head, the heart, and the hara—is considered by many to be an energy center.

The head is the center for mental clarity.

The heart is the center for openheartedness, kindness, gratitude, and forgiveness.

The hara is the center for strength, stability, and perseverance.

In other words, when we put our attention in each center, it is a way to help develop the qualities associated with that center—the clarity of the head center, the openheartedness of the heart center, and the strength and stability of the hara center.

WE START with adjusting our posture, being sure that we're sitting up in an erect and alert position.

NOW BRING your attention to the breath, letting the breath breathe at its natural rhythm.

It doesn't matter if it's fast or slow or irregular—just let the breath breathe itself.

NOW FOCUS on the head center, on the spot right above the bridge of the nose, midway between your eyes.

Place two fingertips there, and for the next five breaths, as you breathe in, focus your attention right where your fingers are.

On the out-breath, simply breathe out.

Breathing in and out through the nose, let the breath naturally go a little deeper and slower with each breath.

NOW MOVE your attention to the center of your chest—the heart center.

Place your fingertips there, and for the next five breaths, as you breathe in, focus your attention right where your fingers are.

Breathing in and out through the nose, again let the breath naturally go a little deeper with each breath.

NOW MOVE your attention to the abdomen—the hara—around two inches below the navel.

Place your fingertips there, and for the next five breaths, as you breathe in, focus your attention right where your fingers are.

Breathing in and out through the nose, again let the breath go a little deeper with each breath.

NOW RETURN to the head center, on the spot right above the bridge of the nose, midway between your eyes.

For just three breaths, as you breathe in, focus your attention right on the head center.

NOW MOVE your attention back to the center of your chest—the heart center.

For just three breaths, as you breathe in, focus your attention right on the center of the chest.

. . .

Now move your attention to your abdomen—the hara—around two inches below the navel.

And for the next three breaths, as you breathe in, focus your attention right on the lower belly.

Now let's return again to the head center, on the spot midway between your eyes.

Stay there for just one breath.

Then one breath to the center of the chest—the heart center.

Then one breath to the abdomen—the hara.

Continue repeating this cycle of one breath to each center for a couple of minutes. You can use your fingertips if it helps.

If your mind starts to wander, you can use this simple mantra: "Head, Heart, Hara"—staying with each word for one breath, and directing your attention to the place the word is pointing to.

Now try to feel all three areas—the head, the heart, and the hara—at the same time.

On the in-breath you can go quickly from the head to the heart to the hara, spending around one second at each point.

Breathing into that whole area, let the breath take you deeper into the whole of yourself.

. . .

Again, on the in-breath, bring your attention to the whole area between the head, heart, and hara.

On the out-breath, just breathe out.

Continue focusing on all three areas on the in-breath for the next few minutes.

You may have to practice this for a while to get the full effect—of feeling alert and centered and more conscious.

Meditation, at its best, is a serene inhalation of what is most real, with an exhalation filled with gratitude and kindness.

THREE BREATHS—A CONSCIOUS PAUSE

One simple but very effective technique to help us on the path of conscious living is called the Three Breaths Practice. Normally, there are many times throughout the day when we "come to," when we simply become aware.

Unfortunately, most of the time, these moments last only a few seconds; afterward, we fall right back into waking sleep, where we are basically unaware, lost in our thoughts or our personal drama. The Three Breaths Practice is a way of helping to extend these moments of awareness, not just during meditation, but throughout our day-to-day living.

The Three Breaths Practice involves injecting a conscious pause in the middle of our usual state of waking sleep, a pause that lasts for the duration of three full breaths. Here's how it works: whenever you "come to" for a moment, make the *conscious intention* to stay there for at least three full breaths.

You don't necessarily focus just on the breath itself,

but bring awareness to your entire experience in that moment, *whatever* it may be.

FOR EXAMPLE, IF YOU "WAKE UP" in the midst of impatience, you don't try to become patient. You simply feel—*fully feel*—the visceral texture of the present moment experience, impatience and all. The commitment is to reside in the experience for the duration of three full breaths.

THERE'S A VERY definite sensation of being present that can be cultivated by the Three Breaths Practice. Try this brief experiment: First, bring attention to your breath, feeling the coolness as it enters the nostrils. Staying with the sensations of the breath, now bring awareness to the overall experience of the body. And staying with the breath and the body, also experience the room.

Don't focus on specific sensations, but instead on the overall or gestalt feeling of the body in space, the sense of your own presence, or being, just sitting there, breathing and being in the room.

Now stay with this, with as much of your attention as you can bring, for three full breaths. If you can do this, you'll recognize the experience as one of being present, of being here, in the sense of expanding beyond your customary limiting perceptual boundaries.

ONE OF THE reasons the Three Breaths Practice is so helpful is that it's something you can actually do without a strong or prolonged effort. It's brief and simple; something you can do many times throughout the day, regardless of how you are feeling.

We all know that it's not enough to simply *want* to wake up; the forces of sleep are powerful and unrelenting. Yet, this one simple practice, which is often not particularly difficult, can begin to bring moments of clarity and presence to our normal fog of waking sleep.

JUST SETTLE into the moment and remind yourself to *feel this*—for at least three full breaths.

28

SHOCKS AND RETURNING TO REALITY

Sometimes, to become aware, we have to be jolted out of our protective shell. Sometimes the repeating shocks of life's disappointments momentarily wake us up to what we normally cannot see.

Part of the path of self-realization is about learning how to receive these shocks: the things we don't like, the person who criticizes us, the job that goes wrong, the mate who leaves us, the health that fails us—whatever shakes us up.

Being jarred awake from our daily waking sleep is no different from being awakened from our nightly sleep. How do we wake up from our nightly sleep? We use alarm clocks to jar us into wakefulness. The shocks we receive from life's disappointments are like alarm clocks in that they pull us out of sleep into reality.

But there's another kind of alarm clock, one that doesn't come from life's lessons. This alarm clock is one that we ourselves consciously set up to specifically counter the unrelenting force of our mechanical conditioning. We set it up to jar us out of our self-centered dream.

An example of this type of alarm clock is *taking pauses in time.* Pauses in time are prearranged signals that we use to wake ourselves up, to bring us back to *just being here.*

One of my own "pauses in time" is the telephone ringing. Whenever the phone rings, instead of picking it up right away, I always let it ring twice. Even though I might want to answer it right away, I just sit there and feel the breath in my chest center as it rings twice.

I'm not trying to do anything, like getting calm or centered. I'm just feeling the breath and the heart and noticing where I am, being present to the moment. Then I pick up the phone. One virtue of this particular practice is that its occurrence is so unpredictable. Since we never know when the phone will ring, it catches us in all of our craziness.

Pauses in time can be very effective for a few weeks or months—but then we might tune them out altogether. A good example of this is the picture I put in my entry hall of the young girl ice skating. She's seemingly carefree, while right in front of her is a sign that says, "Beware, Thin Ice." I put this picture right where I would pass by it every day, and for the first several weeks it worked as the perfect alarm clock. I'd smile whenever I saw it, because it would remind me in a lighthearted way of how much time we spend skating on thin ice, sliding through life oblivious to what we eventually have to face. It's one of my favorite practice themes. Seeing the picture would wake me up to the moment, providing that pause in time where I could just experience being present.

Sometime later, I realized that I hadn't looked at the

picture for weeks. Even though I'd probably walked by it several hundred times, I hadn't seen it at all! As we begin to see this happen with practice alarm clocks, we see the power of the waking sleep-state.

In my early years of practice, when I would "fail," say, by no longer seeing the picture, I'd condemn myself for being on the wrong track, or for not being up for the task. At some point, I finally understood that we can't wake up simply because we want to. We may want to with great fervor one moment, but our basic mechanicalness will predictably and inexorably arise to counter our aspiration.

Thus, we must invent one alarm clock after another, whatever it takes to awaken ourselves from the incredibly limiting self-centered dream. We change the picture, move it to another wall, turn it upside-down, or do whatever we have to do so that the alarm clock will do what it is intended to do: wake us up.

We seem to almost be wired not to see how caught up we are in our usual state of waking sleep. This is why perseverance is an essential quality on the path of self-realization—without it we would most likely just give up.

PART III

29

PATTERNS, CONDITIONING, AND THE PATH

A while back, I was interviewed for a Buddhist magazine, and the interviewer asked me lots of questions about my past, my personal history, and even my interests. At first, I thought most of this was useless. My thought was, "Who cares about whether I was once Jewish or that I play the drums or once lived in a commune?"

But then I started to see what he was looking for. He was trying to see how my conditioning and my personal patterns, especially the things I struggled with, led me to my present views of the path of self-realization, and particularly to what I emphasize as a teacher.

I generally don't like to look for explanations for how I feel right now by analyzing what happened in the past. I see the need to analyze primarily as a dodge, to avoid feeling the discomfort we don't want to feel in the present.

I also believe that our explanations are, at best, only marginally accurate. We've forgotten much more than we remember, and much of what we remember is like window dressing in a shop—putting forth one thing in the foreground and putting something else in the background, all the while creating an interesting or compelling picture of "Me," a picture that may have very little relationship to my actual life.

AND YET, in spite of my skepticism, as I started to answer his questions, I began to understand my own patterns in a new way. For example, there is no doubt that I was born with a predilection toward seeing my cup as half empty. Given this psychological predisposition as a No-Sayer, it makes sense that the decisions I made about life early on would follow the basic philosophy of "Life is too hard. I can't do it."

But conditioning can take strange twists. For example, instead of staying stuck in my pessimistic stance, which could have easily been reinforced by a three-year period of intense illness, I came out of that experience with a very different life view.

It wasn't that I went from a half-empty to a half-full disposition—both are equally conditioned stances. It was the inner realization that the essence of freedom is in saying Yes to life. And by that I don't mean we have to like our difficulties, but that we're willing to experience them as what's actually going on in the moment.

Saying Yes to our difficulties also means that we understand that they're our exact path to freedom.

So instead of following my psychological or conditioned disposition to say No, I learned to say Yes—not just as an affirmation, which is usually just a mental overlay, but as my inner response to difficulties.

How did this very significant change happen? There's a part of me that wants to interpret this in romantically spiritual terms—that through my suffering, my innate wisdom guided me toward the path of truth and equanimity.

But honestly, I can't say. I can't ignore that the very same experiences could have easily taken me in a much different direction. Nonetheless, even if I can't put my finger on the whys and hows, there's no question that my present view of life was very much shaped by my specific struggles.

This is why, as a teacher, I place so much emphasis on seeing our difficulties as our path, and on learning what it means to say Yes to them.

ANOTHER OF MY paths has been my relationship to fear. Since anxiety had been my almost constant companion in so much of my early life, for many years my main motivation in practice was to become free from the discomfort of anxiety and fear.

But after unsuccessfully trying to rid myself of fear, I was drawn to the seeming simplicity of Zen meditation, with the hope that if I sat long enough and hard enough, my fears and other persona issues would resolve on their own, without the need to struggle against them.

This was not to be! In my early years in Zen, the practice emphasis was on staying with the breath in a very concentrated way. And although I had many wonderful experiences of absorption from this practice, I gradually learned that, unfortunately, it also shut much of life out. That doesn't make it a bad practice—it's just limited. And my fears remained intact.

After I saw the limitations of exclusively doing a concentrated breath practice, I started doing a version of wide-open awareness, and continued with it for several years. The instruction was to let go of troublesome thoughts and feelings, and at the time this seemed to make sense. But gradually, I realized that I was still ignoring the fears that needed to be addressed.

Whether we sit in absorption of the breath or in a sense of spaciousness, the belief that if we sit long enough, we will automatically become free from the attachment to our beliefs and fears, is closer to wishful thinking than the truth.

All we have to do is look at the recent history of various meditation traditions to see the folly of ignoring our psychology. Closer to home, all I had to do was look at myself! When my Pandora's box of fear opened up, and the instruction was to "just sit," or to "just let it go," it became obvious that something was missing.

This is what led me to conclude that it is necessary to include the Me-stuff—our beliefs, emotions, and fears—as an essential part of spiritual practice. These aspects, which seem to be embedded in our bodily or cellular memory, have to be addressed directly, as the physical experience of our life.

My present understanding of meditation practice is very much based on my disappointments from following approaches that don't include clarifying the nature of emotions and thinking. Although I still find much of value in the traditional approaches, now when I meditate, my main intention is to be present with *whatever* is there, including what we normally view as the "bad" stuff.

I'm not talking about indulging the repeating stories, but in observing them and staying with the physical experience, rather than trying to let them go. Of course, this is only a part of what spiritual practice is, but it's a part that can't be ignored, as much as we might like to ignore them.

For example, if anxiety arises while I'm sitting in meditation, I don't try to override it by intensely following the breath. Rather, I ask what the believed thoughts are, and immediately go to the physical experience of anxiety in the body. The thought may be "Life is too hard," while the body component may be tightness in the stomach and a rapid heartbeat. The approach is to go back and forth between the thoughts and the bodily experience—not judging it, not trying to let it go, but just staying present with it. Most often, when doing this, the anxiety becomes more porous and light on its own.

THE ONE OTHER path that has become clearer to me relates to my present view on the necessity of cultivating loving kindness as an essential aspect of the path of self-realization.

In my early years in practice, I lived in a Gurdjieff community, and even though I found the Gurdjieff work very helpful, after around seven or eight years I became dissatisfied with what seemed to me like an emphasis on self-perfection, on struggling against what were regarded as flaws or weaknesses in oneself.

Unfortunately, I did plenty of that, and what I found was that whenever we see ourselves as the enemy, we are not only solidifying the persona, we also make practice too serious and almost grim. There was very little of the heart quality of compassion and loving kindness.

When I moved to Zen practice, there didn't seem to be this same emphasis on self-perfection, but it gradually became clear that it was, in fact, still there, just in a more subtle form. The seemingly implicit message is that we need to feel, or be, a particular way—more Zen-like, such as detached or spacious or clear.

This message subtly reinforces our deep-seated self-judgment: that we are not okay as we are. This didn't become obvious to me until my intense period of illness, where I could no longer "measure up" as a disciplined Zen student.

This is also where I discovered the great benefit of doing heart-related practices, such as the loving kindness meditation, which allowed me to directly tap into a deep sense of compassion for myself and my predicament, as well as compassion for others.

This direct approach to loving kindness seemed to have been left out of the Japanese Zen tradition I was initially trained in. Loving kindness, mercy, and compassion were seen as qualities that will come forth naturally, on their own, as we mature in practice. Although this is somewhat true, in many other traditions this aspect is considered something that needs to be cultivated directly.

So, I went outside of my Zen tradition and learned this softer approach to practice from Stephen Levine and Pema Chödrön. I've been doing my own version of the loving kindness meditation literally every day for over thirty years, blending this openhearted quality with the many substantial practices I still find valuable, from both my Gurdjieff practice and my Zen training.

What I've found is that this combined approach seems to be an accelerated path to undercutting the solidity of the judgmental mind, the mind that judges self and others so mercilessly. As a consequence, I believe it allows us to relate to ourselves and others with increasing lightheartedness and kindness.

Although initially skeptical about reflecting on my karmic path, it has nonetheless been valuable in seeing my life journey in a broader perspective. It has also helped me in my teaching—helping me be more empathic toward the struggles of students, and trusting that their struggles, just like mine, would help them gradually learn to stand on their own two feet.

30

LETTING BE

The sense that we can *do* something to guarantee that things will be better is a deeply engrained quality of our life of waking sleep.

The basic understanding on the path of self-realization is that no matter what we bring in the door or how we may be feeling, all we need to do is feel the texture of whatever we're experiencing and then let it be.

Several years ago, during a long period of intense illness, I had to have a blood test every week. From my own early conditioning, I had developed a strong aversion to blood tests; often I'd get dizzy and sometimes I would even faint. My aversion wasn't rooted in fear of pain; it was simply a particular by-product of my own conditioning. The fact that I saw this clearly didn't matter; I'd still go to the tests with lots of anxiety.

In coping, I tried all of the Zen practices I had learned through the years. For example, I'd go in for the blood test and focus totally on my breath. But I'd still faint. Or

I'd say little mantras about spaciousness or about sitting there like a mountain, but it didn't make any difference. Practicing like this to counteract what I perceived as weakness in myself may have even made things worse. In judging myself as "weak," I gave my conditioned reaction even more power.

But one day while driving to the lab, I remembered the practice I had recently learned: to ask, "What is this experience?" to whatever presented itself. From the moment I sat in the chair to have my blood drawn, I kept this practice question before me, intent on experiencing the texture of the moment. When the dizziness began, instead of the anxiety and dread of aversion, I actually felt the excitement of curiosity. I was going to discover what fainting really felt like!

However, I didn't faint. The dizziness passed and I sat there quite at ease. When I gave up the struggle, not only did the unnecessary suffering disappear, but the physical experience transformed as well.

Remember, I wasn't doing this practice in order to avoid the unpleasantness of fainting, which is how we often skew our efforts to become inwardly free. That's what I had been doing before. In this case, by the willingness to just be there, the circuitry of my conditioning was simply disconnected.

I'M NOT TALKING about calling our conditioning an empty illusion and pretending to let it go. That wouldn't be real. What I'm talking about is a certain lightness of heart that we can bring to our experience. Without our attempts to be spacious, spaciousness arises. It arises when we stop believing our judgments, especially the hard-hearted ones we make of ourselves.

When we stop resisting what is, and over time learn the willingness to be with it, it's possible that we will even enjoy our repeating patterns, our little human drama, the whole passing show.

DURING THE EXPERIENCE with the blood tests something clicked, and I realized the depth of my misunderstanding. Although I can try to push away my experience, the fact remains that whatever is happening right now is my genuine life. Like it or not, want it or not, this life is what is.

To embrace it, say Yes to it, rather than push it away, is the key to freedom.

Understanding this allowed me to experience, once again, what it means to cease resistance to what is. With this understanding, I became willing to affirm that I was on board. Whether I liked the trip or not, I would take the ride to see what it was like and where it was going, without the extra baggage of self-pity and fear. Self-pity, fear, the complaints—all of the judgments—are the real obstacles to surrendering to what is.

WHEN WE BEGIN SITTING in meditation, it is always good to start with the question "What is going on right now?" —becoming aware of the state of the body, as well as our mental and emotional state.

The basic theme for meditation—no matter what we bring in the door, no matter how we may be feeling, either physically or emotionally—is to simply sit here and let it be.

To remember that no matter what may be happening

with us, it doesn't have to be seen as an obstacle or an enemy, or something to fix, or change, or get rid of.

In fact, from the point of view of our wish to become inwardly free, whatever it is, it's our path. So, the theme is to simply let it be.

This is not a passive or pseudo-detachment; we still need the discipline to stay present, to stay still, and especially, to choose in each moment not to spin off, and to be precise in our self-observation.

What is being described is an attitude of mind that's just willing to look—to really just ask, "What is this experience?"—to whatever arises. To simply want to know, to be with, to reside in, the truth of the moment.

We can enter the silence of meditation not by trying to enter, but through the constant soft effort to let life be.

When we sit in meditation, struggling is always optional.

"Suffering" also, in a way, is optional.

Instead, we can just observe it, experience it, and then let it be.

This is about a certain lightness of heart that is possible to bring to our meditation—a certain sense of spaciousness—a willingness to cease all of our hard-hearted judgments about ourselves. Basically, ceasing resistance to what is.

Sometimes we may have anxiety. The practice is to feel it, hear the thoughts, and just let it be there.

Sometimes we may be tired or sleepy. The practice is to really feel that, and then to just let it be there.

Sometimes we may feel resistance, or feel discouraged in our sitting. The practice here is, again, to truly feel and experience that resistance or discouragement, and then to simply let it be there.

Whatever self-beliefs arise, such as "I'm just too tired" or "This is too painful" or "I can't do this" or "I will never be good at this," if we can just notice them for what they are, and then just let them be—instead of believing in them as the truth—we can begin to soften around our judgmental mind, and to come to see that these negative self-beliefs are not the deepest truths about ourselves.

We can then begin to relax into our meditation—essentially, relax into our life.

And perhaps even get a glimpse of the profound yet simple truth that all we really need to learn is the willingness to just be.

31

WHAT IS OUR LIFE ABOUT?

There are many obstacles to being willing to just be.

A student walked in to see the meditation master. Sitting down, he blurted out, "There's something terribly wrong with me!" The master looked at him and asked, "What's so wrong?" The student, after a moment's hesitation, responded, "I think I'm a dog." To that the master responded, "And how long have you thought that?" The student replied, "Ever since I was a puppy."

What does this story have to do with spiritual practice? The answer is—everything! It puts the basic human problem in a nutshell. Next time you find yourself immersed in the drama of a strong emotional reaction, awash with deeply believed thoughts, ask yourself how long you've taken these thoughts to be the truth. Especially notice the ones you believe the most: "Life is too hard," "No one will ever be there for me," "I'm worthless," "I'm hopeless." How long have you believed these thoughts? Ever since you were a puppy!

These deeply held beliefs may not be visible on the

surface of our minds; we're often not even aware of them. Yet we cling to such deep-seated beliefs, these basic identities, because they've become rooted in our very cells—in our cellular memory. And their imprint on our lives is unmistakable.

But in order to avoid experiencing the painful quality of these beliefs and identities, we continually engage in various strategies of behavior—habitual coping patterns that buffer us from the anxious quiver of insecurity. These strategies are our attempt to establish some sense of safety, security, and familiarity.

THE ONE QUESTION that we rarely ask, and the one that goes directly to the heart of the matter, is "What is my life really about?" The degree to which we can be honest in answering this question will determine our clarity in understanding the basic human dilemma—that we are cut off from awareness of our own true selves.

For example, how much of the day are you aware—just basically aware of what life is presenting—rather than being lost in waking sleep, in being identified with whatever you're doing, almost as if you didn't exist?

To what extent do you just blindly drift from one form of comfort to another, from one daydream or fantasy to another, from one secure place to another, in order to avoid the anxious quiver of discomfort or insecurity?

How much of your energy is used to fortify a particular self-image, or to simply please others in order to gain approval?

More specifically, can you see the particular ways in which you attempt to avoid really being with your life? Do you know which strategies you use to guarantee some sense of safety and familiarity, to avoid facing the fears—of rejection, loss, unworthiness, or failure—that lie beneath the surface of your thoughts and actions?

THE ESSENCE of the path of self-realization involves cultivating awareness. This process has two basic aspects. The first is clarifying the mental process. The second is experiencing—entering into awareness of the physical reality of the present moment.

The practice of clarifying the mental process entails seeing through our deeply believed thoughts and most basic identities in all aspects of our lives. The point is to see that these beliefs and identities have become so solidified—as if it's *always* been this way—that we take them as truth.

As well, we have to see how our behavioral strategies, which always arise out of fear-based core beliefs, have become so conditioned that they, too, seem like the truth of our being.

As we see these thoughts and strategies clearly, we also have to deal with the pain that's imbedded beneath them in our cellular memory; and we can do this only through the process of *experiencing*. By bringing awareness to the physical sensations of the present moment, we can spark the transformation of our life of waking sleep into a life that is more alive and genuine.

Paradoxical though it may seem, this transformation will happen only when we stop trying to change ourselves. In fact, trying to change is often the crux of the problem.

We enter into the process of experiencing not in order to change, but to leave the thought-based world and instead connect with the reality of what is. And as we enter this process, what actually happens?

Experiencing our lives transforms them because it eventually makes transparent the seeming solidity of our self-beliefs. As we connect with the physical reality of the moment, we realize, experientially, that the apparent solidity of this thing we call "Me" is actually a complex of deeply believed thoughts, habitual strategies, ancient memories, and sometimes unpleasant sensations.

It's as if all our thoughts, judgments, emotions, and identities are separate components, bound together into a solid world that we feel and believe is our actual self.

When we truly enter the present moment, we can experience that this apparently solid self is not exactly what it seems. As we stop identifying with the narrow sense of "me," we begin to identify with the wider container of awareness itself.

Looking with a mind that's awake reveals the shimmering pulse of life. Looking with a mind full of thoughts reveals only our thoughts.

I WROTE this poem right before my fiftieth birthday. My intention was to recite it daily in order to rekindle my aspiration and to remind me what our life is really about.

What Is Our Life About?
Our aspiration, our calling,
our desire for a genuine life,
is to see the truth of who we really are—
that the nature of our Being is connectedness
and love,
not the illusion of a separate self
to which our suffering clings.
It is from this awareness
that Life can flow through us;
the Unconditioned manifesting freely as our
conditioned body.

And what is the path?
To learn to reside in whatever Life presents.
To learn to attend to all of those things
that block the flow of a more open life;
and to see them as the very path to
awakening—
all of the constructs, the identities,
the holding back, the protections,
all of the fears, the self-judgments, the
blame—
all that separates us from letting Life be.

And what is the path?
To turn away from constantly seeking comfort
and from trying to avoid pain.
To open to the willingness to just be,
in this very moment,

exactly as it is.
No longer so ready to be caught
in the relentlessly spinning mind.
Practice is about awakening to the true Self;
no one special to be,
nowhere to go,
just Being.

We are so much more than just this body,
just this personal drama.
As we cling to our fear,
and our shame, and our suffering,
we forsake the gratitude of living
from our natural Being.

So where, in this very moment,
do we cling to our views?

Softening around the mind's incessant
judgment,
we can awaken the heart that seeks to be
awakened.
And when the veil of separation rises,
Life simply unfolds as it will.
No longer caught in the self-centered dream,
we can give ourselves to others,
like a white bird in the snow.

Time is fleeting.
Don't hold back.
Appreciate this precious Life.

32

THE PATH OF SELF-REALIZATION

A friend told me about once going to see a famous teacher. He was feeling discouraged because he could never practice consistently. He always seemed to be vacillating between effort and resistance, and he felt that there was something essentially wrong with his practice.

The teacher told him that this kind of vacillation was a universal issue in practice. We try and then we "fail." And then we try again only to "fail" again. Over and over, we try, and then we "fail" again and again. Then, at some point, we learn to go deeper.

The spiritual path is rarely a straight line to a fixed goal; it's almost always a mixture of struggle and integration, of confusion and clarity, of discouragement and aspiration, of feeling failure and going deeper.

Seeing through our deeply held beliefs, dismantling the solid sense of the self, facing our deepest fears, opening into the unknown—how could we even imagine that this wouldn't be a gradual and halting process, with many ups and downs?

Yet, until we find the reality of life that we're all seeking, we'll continue to experience dissatisfaction. This reality can't be pinpointed with words, yet it's more genuine than anything we can speak of. All we can say is that it's *who we really are.*

IT'S important to understand that we don't have to seek our true self, or even any particular state of mind. Wherever you are, *whatever* your state of mind, can be the focus on your path of self-realization.

Any distress you may feel—discomfort, anxiety, or emotional upset—is the path itself. It is the opportunity to awaken to a more genuine life. Our difficulties are always our best teachers.

A friend once told me that she saw three things about herself in assessing her practice: she was addicted to her thinking, she was attached to her emotions, and she didn't want to stay in the present moment for more than a few seconds at a time.

This might sound pretty bad, but is there really any problem with this? At least there's awareness of where we're stuck. What's unfortunate is when we give up because our practice is not meeting our expectations.

ON THE FIRST day of a four-day meditation retreat, a student went in to see the Zen master with whom he had been studying for many years. Sitting at the teacher's feet, he asked, "Can you tell me how I'm doing in my practice?" The Zen master thought for a minute, then said, "Open your mouth." The student opened his mouth and the teacher peered in and said, "Okay, now bend your head down." The student bent his head down and the

Zen master looked into his hair, then said, "Okay, now open your eyes really wide." The student opened his eyes and the Zen master glared into them and said, "You're doing fine," and then he rang his bell.

Because the teacher rang his bell, the student had to leave. The next day he returned, quite perplexed by what had happened the day before. "I asked you how I was doing in my practice yesterday and you made me open my mouth, then bend my head, and open my eyes. What did all that have to do with my practice?" The Zen master bowed his head in thought. Then he said, "You know, on second thought, you're not really doing very well in your practice, and the truth is, I am not sure you are ever going to make it." And again, he rang his bell.

The student walked out. You can imagine how confused and angry he felt. The next day he went back, still fuming, and said, "What do you mean, I'm not going to make it in my practice? Do you know that I sit in meditation for an hour every day? Sometimes I sit twice a day. I come to every retreat. I have really deep experiences. What do you mean I'm not going to make it?" Again, the master just sat there, apparently thinking. Then he said, "Well, maybe I made a mistake. Perhaps you are doing pretty well after all." And again, he rang his bell.

There was one more day in the retreat. The student went back to see his teacher, utterly exhausted. He felt distraught and confused, but he was no longer fighting it. He said to the master, "I just wanted to know how I was doing in my practice." This time the teacher looked at him and without hesitation, in a very kind voice, said, "If you really want to know how you're doing in your practice, just look at all of your reactions the last few days. Just look at your life."

. . .

Just look at our life. Unless we begin to connect with the rest of our life, our practice—however strong, calm, or enjoyable—ultimately will not be satisfying.

We all want to change, to make our lives better. But most transformative changes are slow and almost imperceptible. Sometimes we don't even notice the ways practice erodes our habitual protective strategies until one day we find ourselves in a situation that always made us anxious and the anxiety is now gone.

The real measure of how we're doing is the degree to which, little by little, we can find that place where we're closed down in fear, and allow ourselves to stay there and face it.

This takes courage, but courage is not about being free from fear; rather it is the willingness to experience our fears. And as we experience our fears, our courage grows.

Each instance of courage can give us the inspiration to bring a little more determination to our practice, allowing us to enter more regularly and deeply into the spaciousness of the heart, especially when self-doubt arises.

33

WABI-SABI

Fundamentally, *Wabi-sabi* is an ancient view of the world that has three basic tenets: first, everything is always changing; second, nothing lasts forever; and third, nothing is ever perfect.

Just consider this moment. Look around you right now. Will anything or anyone you see last forever? Is anything truly perfect?

INTERESTINGLY, beauty in Wabi-sabi is actually based in this imperfection and incompletion. But the sense of beauty comes from *how* we see things more than from *what* we see. When we can clearly see change, impermanence, and imperfection as the true nature of things as they are, there is a beauty in that.

It is a beauty that may sometimes invoke in us a feeling of poignancy, perhaps with a flavor of spiritual yearning.

Fading autumn leaves would be an example. Or falling cherry blossoms. Or the heirloom watch from your grandfather. Or the old jeans made soft and comfortable by frequent wear and washing.

Or even our aging bodies.

PART of the Wabi-sabi understanding is that physical beauty, and also fame, power, and life itself, are fleeting. From this understanding, the mindset of Wabi -sabi suggests a turning away from the world where we waste our life trying to win, trying to please, trying to look good, trying to be right, trying to prove our worth.

Instead, there is an emphasis on finding the spiritual richness found in living a simpler and more genuine life —if possible, closer to nature. When we can lift ourselves above the compulsion of our to-do lists and our mindless activities, choosing instead to live simply, we may momentarily see the wonder that is always right in front of us.

ANOTHER WAY TO look at this is: to be human means to be born, to live a human life—with our many, many ups and downs, including the gradual breaking down of the body —and then, to eventually, inevitably, die. This is the natural order of things.

Many of our problems derive from not understanding and accepting this.

It is part of the natural order of a human life for things to be imperfect.

Everyone has some pain. Everyone has suffering. Everyone will die.

To expect it to be otherwise is a key reason why we suffer with unhappiness.

. . .

On the other hand, to accept imperfection as part of the natural order of things allows us to relate to our many difficulties with a degree of understanding, and perhaps even equanimity.

For example, if we don't believe that life is supposed to go a particular way, namely the way we want it to go, then we are less likely to complain and resist and struggle. We have these reactions because we still expect life to be good, to be comfortable, to be perfect—at least for us.

It also helps to be aware that we don't have endless time, which is an essential part of the Wabi-sabi point of view: that nothing lasts. The recent pandemic has probably made this clear to all of us.

Being aware that we don't have endless time makes it crystal clear that *right now* is all we can ever experience, and all we can ever work with.

To be willing to be present with what our life is right now, even when it might seem difficult, can even lead to the experience of meaningfulness and a quiet joy.

This is expressed in these famous lines from Leonard Cohen:

"Ring the bells that still can ring. Forget your perfect offering. There's a crack, a crack in everything. That's how the light gets in."

Regarding my own difficulties, when I give up my requirement that things be the way I want them to be, I can more easily be with things as they really are, as imperfect as they may seem to be. And in being present with what is, without judgment, I have learned a great deal from those things.

I learned that as strong as the wanting to be right may be, it pales in comparison to living from the heart.

I learned that as much as I may resist wanting to forgive, without forgiveness, there is only the pain of a closed heart.

And most of all, my difficulties have put me back in touch with my deepest priorities: to use my remaining time to learn to live, as best as I can, from kindness, gratitude, and love.

As well, to live with both enjoyment and genuine human connection, as much as possible, before it is too late.

I HAVE BEEN REMINDED over and over again that nothing lasts.

This is the most poignant part of the teaching: that our connection with the people we've grown to deeply care about will someday end. Feeling the ephemeral nature of that connection hopefully makes us appreciate it all the more.

Yet, it is an undeniable fact that our human tendency is to fight the natural process of impermanence and imperfection. For example, most of us don't like looking or getting older or getting sick. We may even believe that if we can cover over our aging, we will no longer feel unhappiness over getting older.

Another view that increases suffering is to believe, when we're caught in a difficult situation, that if we can do something to fix it, everything will be within our control, and then we can be back to normal.

THE MINDSET of Wabi-sabi is the exact opposite of that.

It's about turning away from pretense, denial, and the endless pursuit of control and perfection. Wabi-sabi is a mindset where we long for something more authentic than the smoothest skin or a life that is in our control.

Wabi-sabi does not exactly offer a specific solution to the circumstances of unwelcome change, including pandemics and old age. Nonetheless it offers the possibility of a meaningful life, where we can find a sense of fulfilment from living a life focused on gratitude and kindness. Even for our ephemeral and imperfect lives.

Wabi-sabi also allows us to connect with those around us in more profound ways, because we understand the ephemeral nature of things—that nothing lasts.

When we understand that the imperfections that come along with life are part of the natural order of things, it helps us to experience a certain kind of peace of mind, even within the sadness of loss.

We can experience equanimity when we stop struggling against the foibles in ourselves and others; when we stop struggling against the inevitable passing of time; and when we stop struggling against a universe that is basically indifferent to our personal wishes.

THERE IS a subtle joy in knowing that we and life and everyone and everything are by nature imperfect—and in understanding that that's just how it is. And within awareness of that imperfection, we are more likely to live doing what we love, rather than sleepwalking through life as if we had endless time.

Do we generally live doing what we love? Unfortunately, the answer is no. Just ask yourself if you love what you actually do. Our love needs to be reflected in what we do; otherwise, it is just imagination.

I have found it worthwhile to write down a list of what I love, including people, activities, and experiences —things like cooking and playing Ping-Pong. I regularly look at my list and reflect on my life to see what I'm leaving out. Sometimes even simple things, like listening to my favorite music or spending time at the ocean, can be easily forgotten. But with the understanding that my time is limited, and that I have no idea what is right around the corner, I make sure to include what I might be leaving out in my daily living.

Doing what we love guarantees that we are more likely to experience a life of meaningfulness and joy.

34

LEVELS OF UNDERSTANDING

Everything we observe is in some way related to something else, which in turn is related to something else again. In other words, each element of our life is part of a system, and each system is a part of another system.

No single explanation can ever really explain or even describe the complexity of this interrelatedness. Nor can it take into account the filter of the person who is trying to explain it. Yet we constantly try to figure out our world by categorizing, simplifying, and generalizing.

Furthermore, we think we can experience this world only through our perceptions. But as filtered pictures of a perceived reality, our perceptions are never accurate.

Our bubble of perception is filtered through the mental constructs of time, space, and causality, as well as our personal associations, desires, language, and conditioning. This means that we don't see things as *they* are, we see them as *we* are.

. . .

On a day-to-day level, when what we perceive fails to match our ideas of how things should be, we experience emotional and physical distress. When what we experience is contrary to what we want—and what we want almost always involves being free from discomfort and pain—we experience suffering.

Even though we know we're living in a complex world of interconnections, we tend to focus on just one element of any given situation: Why is this happening to me? Who can I blame? How can I fix it?

When we do this, we reduce the web of interrelationships to a simplified version of an answer we can never really know. We could just as arbitrarily attribute our distress to the potato salad we ate for lunch.

Again, when problems arise in our life, we usually want simple answers—yes or no, this or that. But reality is a world of subtlety and paradox, a world of complexity, continuums, and change. Yet, we are insistent in wanting to know why (why is this happening?) and how (how can I fix it?).

When I look at what's going on in the world around me on a daily basis, most of what I see is grimness and uncertainty, starting with global issues like the climate crisis, the worldwide Covid pandemic, the widespread famines, war-torn countries where daily atrocities occur, the all-too-frequent mass shootings, homelessness, and the political arena where polarization now prevents almost any meaningful compromise on issues that desperately need addressing. All of this adds up to widespread feelings of anxiety and depression.

We want answers. We want the feeling of perceived comfort that comes when we think we've finally figured life out. But the truth is, we'll never figure life out. Again, we'd be better off just to chalk it up to the potato salad, and thus learn what it means to simply reside in the experiential texture of the present moment.

Here is where we learn to reside in the uncertainty we normally try to avoid. However, this does not mean we give up on practical solutions. I still vote. I still contribute to fighting climate change and to the alleviation of world hunger.

BUT IT IS EXACTLY *HERE*, in the midst of uncertainty, that we can find the rock-bottom security that is possible through spiritual practice, as we continue our inner search to experience the truth of who we really are.

It's good to remember: Clear mind does not arise from thinking clearly. Clear mind is what remains when we're not caught by our thoughts.

BUT SEARCHING for the truth is deeply ingrained in us. And in spite of the pitfalls, this search still has some benefits. Searching for the truth may at times entail reading books and listening to teachers. Still, one thing to keep in mind is that there is a big difference between intellectual knowledge and experiential understanding. Intellectual knowledge is when we acquire facts. But for experiential understanding to become real, an idea needs to be processed through our lived experience.

This may sound obvious, but it is actually more subtle than we might think.

Without our efforts, without our inner struggles, without the experiential component, our ideas will remain merely conceptual.

As Nietzsche wrote: "Only thoughts reached by walking have any value." By *walking,* Nietzsche meant *living*.

Many stay stuck here—approaching spiritual practice, largely in an intellectual or conceptual way, without realizing it.

An essential point is that it is up to the student, not the teacher, to take the teachings to a deeper level.

This is subtle: any talk, any practice idea, even the most basic one, can be understood on different levels.

For example, any idea can be understood just as knowledge.

Or, it can be understood on deeper and deeper levels as we process it increasingly through our own experience.

This is necessary for ideas to become transformative.

This is how we move from growth in mere knowledge to growth in what we can call Being.

This does not mean we're seeking a bigger or better "me"—what it means is that we are connecting more fully with who we really are.

HERE'S AN EXAMPLE: Take the idea that we live in a state of waking sleep.

In the early phases of practice, I used to equate being asleep with feeling anxious or confused. We might even have glimpses of getting lost in almost everything—especially in our thoughts and in our emotions.

Or we might experience the unnerving realization that we're like a leaf in the wind—being blown about by ever-changing external circumstances.

This understanding of what it means to be asleep is

very necessary in order to motivate us to practice. But it is only part of the picture.

After I had practiced for a few years, the idea that we are asleep took on a new meaning. But this meaning was a result of my practice, of my self-observations, of my efforts. We may now understand that there are many Me's—that we act out of many different beliefs and self-images housed within the same body.

I remember beginning to see that being asleep meant living out of illusions that I previously was not even aware of. We begin to see the depth of our negative core beliefs, and how much of our life is run by these fear-based beliefs.

At times we may also get a taste of what a real dry spot is, where our motivation to practice literally dries up, and we can begin to see that this dry spot is yet another manifestation of sleep.

As my practice matured further, I began to understand an even more profound meaning of the idea that we're asleep. I got an inner sense of what it means to live as a separate self, to live disconnected from the Heart, from our true nature. I experienced the existential angst of not living genuinely.

This understanding of sleep may only be an intellectual understanding for many years. Only after our struggles to live awake, to face our fears, to practice kindness, will the depth of the human problem of separateness become clear to us.

So, you see, a basic idea, such as the idea that we're asleep, can be understood very differently, depending on our maturity in practice.

. . .

LET'S take another practice idea: the very common instruction that we should stay with the breath.

At first, I understood this as meaning I should stay concentrated just on the breath. And the idea is that if we do this, we will likely become calm. Of course, this is what most of us believe meditation is about in the early phase of practice.

Later, after I had worked with this for a while, I came to a deeper understanding. I moved away from simply trying to become calm to using the breath as a part of a wider container of awareness. The awareness of the breath becomes the space within which we experience our thoughts and emotions, and we are now moving toward cultivating a larger sense of what life is.

But the awareness of the breath can take us even deeper. As I worked with the breath for many years, it became a touch point or portal into reality.

Instead of a disciplined focus on the breath, the awareness is very light. Without effort, we regularly become aware of the breath breathing itself. It's like a breeze that goes right through you.

Paradoxically, it's wonderful, while also being nothing special.

Again, the idea that we can use the breath for awareness can be understood very differently, based on our actual life. These different understandings are not intellectually based, but based on our developing experience.

LET'S take another practice idea—the idea that our difficulties are our path.

In the early years, I understood this idea as meaning that we have to struggle against our difficulties, that we have to go against our flaws.

Specifically, I understood this as meaning I should strive to eliminate my fears, much like a behavior modification program.

Later, when it became clear to me through my struggles that this approach would never work anyway, my understanding of the idea that our difficulties are our path took on a new meaning. I now understood that whether I liked my difficulties or not, these things were *exactly* what I needed to truly experience in order to become free.

This is what it means to say Yes to a difficulty—to truly face and feel what we don't want to feel. But, it's not to get rid of it. We no longer relate to it as the enemy, or as the obstacle that needs to be conquered. Rather, we're willing to experience it as the present moment experience of our life—with a curiosity to explore it and go deeper.

An invaluable part of this evolution is the fact that, while our difficulties may remain, they no longer rule us.

And as we continue to face our difficulties and our fears, an even deeper understanding emerges: the view that our difficulties are actually an important part of our path.

When we can say Yes to our difficulties on this deeper level, we can begin to relate *to* them from a larger sense of what life is. We relate *to* them from the bigger container of awareness, where our attachment to our difficulties becomes much less of an issue. We understand that difficulties are a part of every life, and we even learn to relate to them from loving kindness, looking at our own fears with almost a friendliness or lightness of heart—no longer seeing them as defects.

This is the experience of true equanimity.

. . .

LET'S take one last example: the idea that we need to practice loving kindness.

At first, in the early part of my practice, I used the loving kindness practice to try to feel good—particularly to feel loving or kind. This may be a superficial understanding of the practice, but perhaps we need to go through it, as I did.

Going to a deeper level, we can come to the understanding that the cultivation of loving kindness requires working with whatever blocks our way to it. And as we work in this way with all of our inner fears and barriers, we begin to relate to ourselves in a new way—without so much self-judgment.

For example, we all know how hard we are on ourselves when we have an unwanted emotion or behavior arise. Perhaps we see ourselves as weak or worthless, and loving kindness is the last thing from our minds and hearts.

But as we practice loving kindness, we begin to relate to our fears and our weaknesses as just the all-too-human conditioning that we are all subject to.

But there's an even deeper level that the loving kindness practice can take us to.

It can gradually move from being a specific practice to being our natural response to life. When things happen to us, we begin to extend loving kindness automatically, just like we would to a child in distress. There is a natural warmth or friendliness not only toward ourselves, but also toward others, which makes our life much lighter and free.

In fact, it becomes increasingly difficult to act with unkindness, because we immediately sense that we are disconnecting from the heart, from our True Nature.

But this natural flowing of loving kindness doesn't

come from the mind, or from a "should," or from any intellectual understanding.

It comes from our hard work in learning to go deeper into our practice.

In sum, knowledge and understanding are two very different things.

Knowledge is necessary and useful, but very limited by itself in helping us to actually live more awake. Understanding, on the other hand, which can only develop from the depth of our practice, results in an actual change in our Being.

And with each basic practice idea, as it moves from the level of knowledge to deeper levels of understanding, we can learn to travel the path of self-realization in a new way.

35

HERE ARE SOME ANSWERS TO THE QUESTION "WHAT IS THE PATH OF SELF-REALIZATION?"

You can choose one as a slogan to work with each day. As you go through your day, hold it in your mind and use it to deepen your experiential understanding of what your life is about.

- The path is about being with our life as it is, not as we would like it to be.
- The path is about becoming free of the slavery of our self-judgments and our shame.
- The path is about increasing awareness of who we are and what our life is.
- The path is about learning to be a lamp unto ourselves.
- The path is always about returning to the true self.
- The path is about the growing ability to say "thank you" to everything that we meet.
- The path is about the clash between what we want and what is.

- The path is about increasingly entering into Love—not personal love, but the Love that is the nature of our Being.
- The path is about turning from a self-centered view to a life-centered view.
- The path is about willingly residing in whatever life presents to us.
- The path is about appreciating our preferences without making them demands.
- The path is about perseverance—the ability to continue in our efforts even though life doesn't please us in the ordinary sense.
- The path is about learning to live from the open heart—the heart that only knows connectedness.
- The path is about learning to say "Yes" to what's happening—Yes, I'm willing to experience this in this moment—even when we hate it.
- The path is about giving ourselves to others, like a white bird in the snow.
- The path always comes back to the *willingness to just be.*
- The path is about finally understanding the basic paradox that although everything is a mess, All is Well.

36

MAGNETIC CENTER

Reflecting on our patterns and our personal path, an interesting question to ask is: What draws people to a spiritual path?

Think for a moment: Do you remember what first drew you?

Of course, there may be a variety of reasons why people start a practice, and also why they stay in practice. But one reason worth focusing on is the sense of dissatisfaction that many of us have felt. This is the feeling that something is missing—that there must be more to living than what has thus far been attained.

This is not the desire to have more or be more in the ordinary sense. This is a unique kind of desire. It's a desire to fill an internal longing—a desire to find satisfaction beyond attaining money, security, good health, a family, and so on.

Perhaps you may be feeling something like this now, where life seems vaguely out of synch, without knowing exactly what is missing. It's worth noting that not everyone has this desire for something more. But if we have it, it will drive us.

In one spiritual tradition, this desire was called magnetic center.

In a way, magnetic center is like an inner directedness, a compass that points us, directs us, draws us like a magnet, toward our true north—toward a spiritual path.

Our magnetic center can be very strong, in which case we might begin our spiritual search early in life—usually from a sense of existential disappointment.

Or, if it's not so strong, it could lead us from one thing to another—from yoga, to meditation, to one teacher to another—never really staying with one practice long enough.

Or, staying with a practice but never really making the efforts to go deeper.

Without a fairly strong magnetic center, it is unlikely that we'll be able to persevere through all the difficulties and valleys that are inherent in a spiritual search. It is unlikely that we'll stay when our illusions about practice are dispelled—such as the illusion that practice will take away all of our difficulties.

Interestingly, when I meet students, I never can tell whether or not their magnetic center is strong enough to see them through. In fact, I have been surprised over and over again by students—some who leave practice when I was sure they would stay, and others who I was absolutely sure would leave but instead end up becoming strong students.

So you may wonder: How does one know if one has a strong magnetic center?

One way is through the quality of your discipline and perseverance. Consider yours. If you don't have much discipline and perseverance, it is likely that your magnetic center could use some strengthening.

Another way to assess your magnetic center is through your willingness to go toward the unfamiliar. If you tend to insist on the comfort of the familiar, it is likely a reflection of a tentative magnetic center.

For example, during difficult periods, are you able to adapt to your uncomfortable circumstances and not lose touch with your practice discipline? As well, are you clear about what practice is, with your specific difficulties?

The answers to these questions can be very informative.

Of course, we all have lapses in discipline, and we all seek comfort to some extent. So this is not a cause for our classic default setting of criticizing ourselves as being lacking. But it is something that's worth looking at.

IT'S ALWAYS good to remember that life is not perfect. Imperfection is the natural state of everything, including ourselves. Our capacity to understand this truth will allow us to continue on the spiritual path without getting caught in incessant self-judgment.

But it's also important to understand the kinds of detours that we can take from the true north of our magnetic center.

There is the classic detour of thinking and talking about practice rather than actually practicing. We all do this, but it's a matter of degree.

There is the detour of mistaking complacency for

genuine equanimity. These are the times where we turn away from difficulties—even though we know they can be our best teacher—in order to maintain the comfort of complacency.

Then there is the classic detour of indulging our tendency to blame. We can blame others, the practice, and especially ourselves. However we indulge in blaming, it is *always* a detour from reality.

So is trying to fix what we see as wrong, rather than experiencing what is actually going on in a particular situation.

Our specific detours have to first be seen clearly. Then, once seen, we can start by simply saying "Hello" to them.

Saying "Hello" to them is a way of relating from the heart, with kindness to ourselves; and it allows us to work with them much more effectively.

Taking a detour doesn't mean something is wrong with us—they're just conditioned responses. And as we work with them—meaning, bringing awareness to them —they lose their power, and the magnetic center can then grow.

THE QUESTION NATURALLY ARISES: Is there anything else that we can do to make our magnetic center stronger? And the answer is a definitive yes. We can feed our magnetic center in a variety of ways.

One way, of course, is by reading books and listening to talks. But, as you probably know, this is just preliminary—unless we put what we read or hear into practice, it is not real food for our Being.

We can also regularly remind ourselves of our practice aspiration, as a way of intentionally awakening our magnetic center. Every day before I meditate, I remind myself very specifically why I am meditating.

Regularly being around a group of people who have a similar path is also a definite help, in that it reminds us what is most important to us. It can also bring some energy and discipline that we might not have when we're alone.

Likewise, periodic contact with a teacher is sometimes essential in keeping our magnetic center oriented in the right direction.

BUT PERHAPS THE most important way we feed our magnetic center is through our direct experience. For example, we feed our magnetic center each time we sit in meditation. Each moment sitting, when we can be present to ourselves, is food for our Being.

And when we sit for longer meditation retreats, where we are pushed to make efforts, we may actually feel our magnetic center getting stronger.

The opposite of this is also true: if we don't feed our magnetic center, it will get weaker. When we don't meditate regularly or attend longer retreats frequently enough, we will usually stay in a kind of practice limbo.

Quite a few students over the years have mentioned to me that they felt they were losing touch with their practice, which is another way of saying they were losing touch with their magnetic center. One student, in reflecting on the absence of personal contact, described her practice as feeling like a weak gruel.

But, persevering in a regular sitting practice, even when it feels weak, is still better than doing nothing, and our magnetic center will still be fed enough to help keep us on course.

Sometimes, the events in our lives can temporarily throw our magnetic center off course. When this happens, it's always good to ask yourself, "Why am I on the path of self-realization?" If the answer isn't immediately clear, that's good information to have.

Perhaps it would be useful over the next few days to ask this question. Or if you have a regular meditation or prayer practice, to ask what your aspiration is at the beginning of your session. You don't have to think about it; just let the answer arise from your magnetic center.

Hopefully, a practice like this can help us increasingly move from a self-centered life to a more life-centered one, where we naturally live more from kindness, gratitude, and love.

~

AS WE GET OLDER, we may at times feel a loss of direction or little sense of purpose. We may lose our jobs or productive identities, and we may feel obsolete, as if we don't seem to really matter. Walking down the street, we may feel like we're not even seen.

We will most likely try to use the usual props—keeping busy, entertainments and distractions, even relationships—to cover over the feelings of emptiness inside. But this doesn't feed our magnetic center.

Still, our survival instinct motivates us to find meaning and certainty. This has been described as the existential dilemma: we are beings who search for meaning and certainty in a world that may very well have neither.

. . .

But meaning is certainly possible. And it is possible at any given moment, in exactly what we are experiencing, regardless of whether or not we like it.

There is a definitive and visceral taste of meaning that comes from being present and engaged with whatever our life is.

Being present—truly present—feels inherently meaningful. And genuine equanimity is the natural by-product of experiencing life as inherently meaningful. Being present is also one of the best ways to feed your magnetic center.

When we understand that life is constantly changing, and that both good things and bad things come our way —and that we have very little control—we can learn to accept, be with, surrender to whatever our life is, without demanding that things go any particular way. This allows us to experience the sense of meaning that comes from being truly present and engaged with whatever our life is at any given moment.

But we need to be realistic. I've talked to many students over the years, and made many suggestions to them, but most of the students did very little to really change. At one point, I came to the conclusion that most people don't really want to change. The few who did change, who had a strong magnetic center, usually did so fairly quickly. They really wanted their life to be different, and so they made the effort to make that happen.

What I saw was that the many students who didn't change were, in a way, actually attached to their difficulties. They didn't want to make the effort to give them up. They may even have been waiting for someone to save them.

Of course, no one can save us from our difficulties because the difficulties we're talking about are within us. The students who understood this did not wait for someone or something outside of them to save them; they made the effort, made the choices necessary to turn their lives around.

Our attitudes toward change can differ greatly. There are those who are afraid of it and will do whatever they can to hold onto the status quo, even when they don't necessarily even like it.

Then there are those who look forward to change, seeing it as an escape mechanism. As soon as things get difficult, they are ready to jump to something else.

There are also those who know they need to change but who are afraid to take a step toward the unknown.

And then there are those fortunate enough to have a strong magnetic center—who are willing to make the effort to change, but knowing that we can only do it one little step at a time.

AS STATED EARLIER, life is not perfect. Imperfection is the natural state of everything, including ourselves. Our capacity to understand this truth will allow us to take that one little step without judging ourselves as lacking. And with each little step we take, our magnetic center can grow.

37

REFLECTIONS ON LIVING GENUINELY

We may at least occasionally wonder: What does it mean to live authentically?

We start with the fact that one of the main characteristics of a life of sleep is that we are totally identified with being a "Me." Whether it's our name, our history, our self-images, or our opinions and moods, we use each of these things to solidify the sense that we are living in our little subjective bubble of Me-ness.

We experience ourselves as "special"—not in the normal sense of being distinguished or exceptional, but in the sense that we feel subtly significant. In other words, we feel like a unique and separate self.

The point is, our entire persona system reinforces this interior feeling of Me-ness, uniqueness, specialness.

Interestingly, our feeling of specialness is not just from having positive qualities. We can even use our negative experiences to make us feel unique and special. For example, we can feel special if we're angry or suffering, or if we're sick.

. . .

YET, not *needing* to be special, not needing to be *any* particular way, is what it means to be inwardly free—free to experience our natural being, our most authentic self.

Looking at this in a little more detail, we all have images of ourselves that we unconsciously carry with us throughout our waking hours. Our self-images are the conceptions or pictures of how we see ourselves, and also of how we'd like to be seen.

For example, we can have the self-image of being nice, or competent, or deep; or we could have a negative self-image—seeing ourselves as weak, or stupid, or worthless.

REFLECT on what is your primary self-image—how you'd like to be seen.

Usually, we try to focus on our positive self-images, and we often try to portray ourselves in the most favorable way. The point is: since much of our life is spent trying to live out of our self-images, they become part and parcel of the stories we weave about ourselves.

Yet, these stories are always skewered versions of the truth concerning who we are. By stories I'm including our history, our victimhood, why we're angry, and on and on.

We are caught in a story when we tell ourselves, "I'm worthless," or "I'm depressed," or "People should appreciate me."

We're particularly caught when we say, "I'm this way because . . .," and then assign blame to others such as our parents, or to something that happened to us.

We can also know we're wrapped up in one of our many stories if we have the thought "I'm the kind of person who . . .," or "I'm not the kind of person who . . ."

The point is, most of our stories, just like our self-images, are self-deceptions, in that they are partial truths that we adopt in order to solidify our sense of self. Although it is very difficult to be truly honest with ourselves, we have to understand that living out of stories prevents us from living more genuinely.

Further, every opinion we hold to solidifies this sense of Me. As well as every mood. Every preference. Every aversion. Each of these acts as a filter between us and living authentically.

To be inwardly free means we don't have to live out of our self-images, or our opinions, or our moods. We don't have to believe the stories we tell ourselves—the stories that dictate who we are and how we live.

WHAT DOES it actually look like to live authentically?

First and foremost, living authentically means living with honesty—being willing to look at our own illusions and self-deceptions; questioning our limiting self-images and opinions; examining the stories we weave about ourselves, including our stories about our past and who we think we are.

We have to realize how our self-images, convictions, and stories prop up our sense of purpose and importance, in order to subtly make us feel unique and special —a sense of being a Me.

When we lose one of these props, such as when someone or something we trusted can no longer be counted on, we naturally experience anxiety, because without our familiar supports we are left with just ourselves, which can be a frightening prospect.

. . .

I HAVE a vivid memory from my twenties, when I was zealously involved in a spiritual group based on the teachings of G.I. Gurdjieff. One night I was sitting in a coffee shop in San Francisco, reading a book by some spiritual bigwig. He wrote emphatically that the teacher Gurdjieff was just a small fry, and that his approach really missed the point.

I remember feeling like the bottom dropped out, because at that point I had put all my eggs in this one basket—I believed the Gurdjieff work was going to save me from my anxiety and depression. In other words, I was using it as a prop—to be a somebody that belonged to something special.

I had a similar experience when diagnosed with kidney cancer. This time it wasn't a group that failed me; it was my own body that I could no longer count on. Once again, falling through the thin ice.

When we experience events like these, we often try to regain a sense of control—perhaps by filling our lives with busyness and doing, as well as with our many diversions and entertainments—to guarantee that we are never left alone with ourselves and our fears.

We don't want to feel that hole of emptiness.

BUT AS WE see through our illusions—for example, our illusion of control, or our self-images, or our stories—they decreasingly dictate how we feel and how we live. This is what it means, in part, to live authentically—no longer fooling ourselves with our illusions and self-deceptions.

What this requires more than anything is the courage to be open to our life—being willing to face the things we've never wanted to face. This includes our fears—of pain, rejection, unworthiness, and uncertainty.

To be open, to be present, in turn allows us the possibility of no longer sleepwalking through life—just seeking comfort, security, and approval; and no longer living with the illusion that we are in control, or that we have endless time.

IN ASPIRING to live more authentically, it's also important that we cultivate kindness toward ourselves for the many times that we will, in fact, falter. This includes those times when we *don't* look at ourselves with honesty, or when we waste time instead of meditating, or holler at somebody just because we're in a bad mood.

On the long path of self-realization, we move from living from our self-images and our many stories to living more in the "natural monastery"—from our deepest values, our most authentic self.

WHEN I REFLECT on the teachers I have most admired, the values that stand out the most are honesty in looking at one's life; not settling for complacency; living with presence, inner quiet, and inner strength; and living with appreciation and kindness—all of which contribute to the true contentment of living in the natural or inner monastery.

What gets in the way of this movement toward our authentic self, more than anything, is our insistence on identifying with the small self—preserving our narrow world of being a "Me"—of needing to look and feel a particular way.

. . .

One of my favorite aphorisms goes, "Dropping our facades, our identities, our stories—what remains? The answer: just Being."

Unfortunately, we can't let go of our stories or moods or images just because we want to.

But we can ask ourselves: "Who would I be without this story?"

Right now, close your eyes and focus like a laser on the subjective experience of living in the narrow inner sphere of "Me-ness."

What does it actually feel like, very specifically, to be holding onto an opinion or an attitude, or to be caught in a self-image or a mood?

The practice is to feel the totality of this with as much intensity as possible, allowing the cocoon that protects us, the hard shell that covers the heart, to begin to break open.

When we can enter into this sometimes dark place fully, something else emerges—our natural Being.

Likewise, when we bring awareness in this way to our cherished self-images, such as our need to be special, they begin to lose their power over us.

No longer puffing ourselves up or trying to stand out means we no longer feel the inner compulsion to see ourselves or be seen in a particular way—there is no ulterior agenda.

The result is the experience of no one special to be.

To be no one special means we are becoming psychologically free of the illusion of "I-as-a-Me"—no longer seeing ourselves as a unique self, independent of the world around us.

NOT HOLDING on to any particular view or mood, or the stories about our past and who we are, or the many self-images we use to define our "Me"—what remains? Again, the presence of just Being.

This gives us an experiential taste of our most authentic self, with the inner knowing that who we truly are—our basic connectedness—is more than just our self-images, our stories, even our body.

As awareness opens up, the objective fact of our basic connectedness becomes more than just an intellectual understanding.

Living in the natural monastery, we no longer have to maintain the burden of our stories and self-images, and we can experience the freedom of a simpler life. We can start to do what we love instead of what we think we're supposed to do. We can learn what it means to truly "enjoy the ride."

38

REMEMBERING THE BARRIERS

The first barrier on the path of self-realization is misunderstanding the magnitude and power of what is called "waking sleep." The term "waking sleep" describes the state in which we spend most of our waking hours—where we are identified with, or lost in, whatever is happening.

THE SECOND BARRIER we encounter on the path, closely related to the first, is underestimating the degree to which resistance is a predictable and inevitable part of a spiritually based life.

Resistance is not the same thing as being passive or lazy. We can be busy and productive and still be quite resistant—resistant in the sense that we don't want to honestly look at ourselves and what we're doing.

Resistance comes in many forms: not wanting to sit in prayer or meditation; choosing to spin off into our mental world; suppressing or avoiding emotional pain; finding fault with ourselves; finding fault with others.

Another, more subtle form of resistance is thinking and talking about the spiritual path rather than actually experiencing our life.

We spend much of our lives trying to just get along, hoping for our little share of happiness. Unfortunately, this guarantees that we'll end up living primarily from the smallness of our attachments and from the slavery to our fears.

THE THIRD MAJOR barrier we encounter on the spiritual path is our deep-seated desire to feel a particular way, whether it's calm or clear or spacious or simply free of anxiety.

We should never underestimate the extent to which we equate feeling better with being awake. But a key point about spiritual practice is that we don't have to feel *any* particular way.

PLEASE REMEMBER: When we feel discomfort or anxiety, we almost always think that something is wrong. The immediate tendency is to pursue our conditioned strategies—trying harder, hiding, or seeking escape—hoping that we can gain control and get away from the discomfort or anxiety.

But the mere fact that we feel anxious doesn't necessarily mean that something is wrong. The only thing it means is that we're feeling anxious. In other words, we're simply having a conditioned response.

It's very difficult for us to accept the reality that life is not subject to our control—that it is always changing. Much of our suffering arises when we resist this reality.

The inherent groundlessness of life as it is—of the

changing and impermanent nature of things—makes us feel very uncomfortable. Thus, we try mightily to put ground under our feet.

We pretend we're in control, in the same way that the steersman in a rowboat thinks he's in control of his boat. He moves his rudder, and to some extent he can determine where his boat will go. But he forgets that the stream is going at its own speed and that there may well be unknown twists and turns and rapids ahead. Like him, we may occasionally realize that we're not in control, but as soon as our boat hits the quiet waters, we fall back into the illusion that we can control what happens. We simply don't want to feel the uncertainty and groundlessness that this illusion attempts to cover over.

When we experience the discomfort of groundlessness, and especially the feeling of panic when things go really awry, our little mind will naturally resist. It will tell us to fix it right now or to find a sense of ground or some escape.

BUT STAYING on the path of self-realization asks us to view the discomfort, even the panic, with a curiosity that's willing to explore exactly what we're feeling in the present moment. This is what it means to surrender—to simply want to know *what* our life is, whether it's interesting or boring, pleasant or unpleasant, joyful or painful.

Perhaps we should first ask, "What does it actually mean to surrender?" Surrender means, very specifically, to cease fighting—to give up. But give up what?

First, give up our resistance, including our constant effort to avoid discomfort. Surrender also requires that we give up our stories, such as our stories about how our life should be comfortable or within our control, or our stories about how awful things are—stories that are invariably about "Me" and "Mine."

Surrender ultimately means giving ourselves up completely to what is.

When we can enter into this sometimes dark place fully, something else emerges. Tibetan Buddhist meditation teacher Pema Chödrön wrote, "Only to the extent that we expose ourselves over and over to annihilation can that which is indestructible in us be found."

The grace that can flow from consciously experiencing our pain becomes a gift that transcends our imagined helplessness.

The specific practice is to move toward, and to fully reside in, the physicality of our discomfort, allowing the fear, the sadness, the grief, to be breathed directly into the center of the chest.

In the darkest circumstances, breathing into the heart is the one thing that will always be a genuine response to the moment.

Using the breath as a conduit, it's *as if* we're breathing the swirling physical sensations and energy of distress right into the chest center. Then, on the out-breath, we simply exhale. We're not trying to let go of or alter our experience; we're simply using the heart's breath as a container to fully feel our distress.

We can also include the wider sense of the breath—

the air all around us—which gives us a bigger context for experiencing whatever is present.

The point is that the path of the authentic life requires being open to change, to the unknown, to *whatever* arises. Prioritizing safety and control guarantees that our life will remain both very small and very unsatisfying.

Yes, we fear change and discomfort, and we prefer the quiet waters; but in order to live more genuinely, we need be more wary of our desire for comfort and complacency than we are of our fear of change.

WE CAN LEARN that in those moments when our expectations and plans crumble and there seems to be nothing left, it is only by completely surrendering to what is that we can realize that what remains is more than enough.

IN RECENT MONTHS I've had many recollections of my ten years as a hospice volunteer, which began in the early nineties when I was forty-eight. One particular memory was of my second hospice patient, who was close to seventy at the time I met him. He had been quite healthy and was still an active horse shoer in Northern California, when out of the blue he was diagnosed with advanced liver cancer.

He deteriorated very rapidly, and within a few months he was dead. What happened to him is another perfect example of how we're all just one doctor's visit away from falling through the thin ice. The Buddha exhorted us to remember that we are not here forever; he said we should remind ourselves that each day could be our last.

The truth is, we have no idea how long we have, yet we unconsciously assume we have endless time. But if we remember that we have limited time, we can begin to understand that each day is precious and that we waste much of our life replaying the past and worrying about the future.

We can begin, perhaps for the first time, to take our life seriously. We can also begin to truly appreciate the people around us—and the fact that they, too, have limited time.

Do we want to continue our self-centered and small-minded behaviors toward others, when any one of us could die at any time? We certainly wouldn't want someone to die while we were angry at them or filled with petty thoughts and judgments about them.

ONE WAY to viscerally remind yourself of the bigger view is to simply pause, take a long, slow breath, and feel the air enter your body. Then be aware that the air you take in is the same air that is all around you and that, on the exhale, the air inside of you becomes the air outside. We can immediately tap into a taste of the interconnectedness that we are, even if it's on a very small scale.

As a pointer to look deeper, it's important to understand, even conceptually, that we *are* the air we breathe. Just as we each share this air, we share in the life energy that courses through each living thing.

REALITY on this level is vast. To realize our true nature of connectedness means we understand, experientially, that we *are* the vastness, and also, at any given moment, a unique manifestation of it.

This experience, which we can call enlightenment, won't necessarily hit us like a lightning bolt. Most likely it will come gradually, but what does gradual enlightening actually mean?

First, it means becoming increasingly free from the attachment to the prison of our persona, with its deeply ingrained conditioned patterns.

Second, gradual enlightening is where we slowly become free from our very limited bubble of perception.

Normally we think we see reality, but what we see is our own subjective perceptions, filtered through all of our associations and desires, as well as through language and conditioning.

We create this bounded world in order to survive and make sense of things, yet when we live only in our bubble of perception, only in the solid world of fixed boundaries, we are cut off from the totality, the mystery of our being.

The third aspect of gradual enlightening is the long process of becoming free from living with a closed and disconnected heart.

One of the prime sources of experiencing a closed heart is the belief that we *should* be different. Especially after being on the path for a few years, we think we shouldn't still be so reactive. We think we should be beyond our conditioning.

But the path of self-realization doesn't work that way. A more accurate view of what happens on the path is that at first we have a big willful dog on a leash who pulls us along whenever and wherever he wants to go. After many years, we still feel the tug on the leash, and we still hear the dog yapping to go. Our conditioning is still there. But when we look at the dog, we see that it's now just a

Chihuahua. To work with it, all we have to do is let it yap as it will and jerk the leash lightly.

WORKING with the barriers to waking up, learning to surrender to our present moment experience, and learning to live with and accept uncertainty are essential aspects of the gradual path of living a more enlightened life. There is no lightning-bolt experience, no chemical pill, that will permanently transform us. But with the aspiration to live awake and inwardly free, and the perseverance to stay the course despite the obstacles and setbacks, we will eventually begin to taste and enjoy the fruits of the path of self-realization.

39

WHAT IS MOST IMPORTANT

When Elizabeth and I were once in Rome, we came across an old church called Santa Maria della Concezione dei Cappuccini, beneath which lies what's known as the Capuchin Crypt. When the monks arrived there in 1631, they brought three hundred cartloads of the bones of deceased monks and proceeded to arrange the bones in decorative motifs throughout the several underground chapels.

It's quite a sight, but the thing that struck me the most was a phrase on the wall above some of the bones: "What you are now we used to be; what we are now you will be." It was a particularly effective wake-up to what's most important.

I IMAGINE Alfred Nobel had a similar wake-up when he opened the newspaper to find his own obituary in it. It may have been doubly shocking because the obituary stated, "Alfred Nobel, the inventor of dynamite, died this week."

It was actually his brother who had died, but what was most upsetting to Alfred was the realization that he would be remembered for inventing dynamite. The shock of this realization motivated him to reflect on what he considered to be most important.

As a result of his reflections, he sponsored what came to be known as the Nobel Peace Prize. Sobered by reading his premature obituary, he thenceforth put his time, money, and energy into supporting what he valued most —people who were learning to live from the awakened heart, as evidenced by their pursuit of world peace.

When I reflect on what I consider to be the most important thing, the answer I keep returning to is learning to live from the gratitude and kindness of the awakened heart.

Unfortunately, this is not so easy to do; often, to awaken the heart, we first have to experience adversity. We may have to lose things we cherish, where we feel our secure future dissolving right in front of us.

There's a famous story about the wife of a wealthy man whose sorrow was so great when her only child died that she came close to losing her mind. Someone told her to talk to the Buddha. The Buddha told her that he could help her, but first she had to bring him some white mustard seeds from a family where no one had died. She desperately went from house to house, but everywhere she went, someone had died. At first, she was disappointed, but then it struck her that no one was spared the loss of someone they loved.

When she returned to the Buddha, she was able to relate to her sorrow with compassion for others as well as for herself. It was the beginning of moving from self-centeredness to the awakening of the heart.

WHEN WE EXPERIENCE GREAT DIFFICULTY, either on a societal or on a personal level, it often helps break down our self-protectiveness and sense of separation. There are many historical examples on a societal level—from World War II, 9/11, and other times—where people came together in shared purpose and shared heart when faced with overwhelming adversity.

This is certainly true on the individual level as well. When we consciously face our deepest tragedies or suffering, we often feel a sense of connectedness with others who are in pain. Like the woman who went to see the Buddha, we can begin to appreciate our common humanity.

The experience of "my pain" is transformed into "the pain"—the pain all human beings share. This is the essence and definition of compassion.

ONE OF THE most effective catalysts to awakening to what is most important is experiencing the pain of remorse. Sometimes we get a glimpse of the fact that we're living from vanity or unkindness or pettiness, and we feel a cringe of conscience. This is the experience of remorse, which arises when we become acutely aware that we are going against our true nature—against the heart that seeks to awaken.

We can feel the pain we cause others, as well as ourselves; and this experience is almost always sobering. In fact, perhaps as much as anything, the pain of remorse can motivate a profound desire within us to live more awake and more genuinely.

From the pain of deep humiliation—from seeing how we go against our true nature—real humility can awaken.

Several years ago, I had an experience of remorse that had a profound impact on me. While I was sitting on a bench overlooking the ocean doing a loving kindness meditation, a woman who appeared to be homeless came over to talk to me. But after a minute or so I told her I was busy meditating. Do you get it? I was too busy doing a meditation on kindness to extend actual kindness to a person who may have been in need.

As soon as she went away, I felt the shock of remorse. This was not guilt, which is usually based in anger against oneself, but rather the awareness that I'd disconnected from the heart. By allowing myself to truly feel this, to let it etch its way into my awareness without indulging in self-blame, I saw the gap between my ideals about living from kindness and having kindness be a lived reality.

Because the experience of remorse was so intense, it had a residual impact that has stayed with me. Now when I find myself at that choice point between extending myself with kindness or holding back from laziness or self-protection, I am more likely to live from the natural generosity of the heart.

An interesting and sometimes very fruitful exercise in consciously experiencing remorse is to imagine what might be written on your tombstone. Just like the wake-up that Alfred Nobel experienced when he realized he might be remembered as the inventor of dynamite, we can be equally sobered when we see what we might be remembered for.

Would we want our tombstone to say, "He was angry and he died"? Or, "She held on to her resentments until her dying day"? Or, "He died never having given back"?

These may be exaggerations, but we all have big lapses in which we forget what is most important. The point is that we don't have to wait until our death to remember. We can use our "little deaths"—those moments when we see that we're being petty, unkind, or unforgiving—to remind us that the most important thing is to live from the gratitude and kindness of the awakening heart.

I WOULD LIKE my own tombstone to say:

He aspired to give himself to others, like a white bird in the snow.

40

DEATH AS AN ADVISOR

Many of the wisdom traditions consider it crucial to reflect on one's death, and to use death as an advisor to living most fully. These reflections are not meant to be morbid; quite the contrary, they are meant to bring joy into whatever life we have remaining.

RIGHT AFTER MY SEVENTY-SECOND BIRTHDAY, I wrote this short piece:

Daily Reflection on Death
I know I am going to die.
I don't know when or where or how,
yet it's an inescapable fact
that my life will someday surely end.

During the process,
there may be physical pain,
emotional distress, or mental decline.

But however it unfolds, the fact remains:
everything that I am will no longer be;
everyone that I care about will no longer be;
all that I do will no longer be.

This, right now, will no longer be.
Nor will my pains and fears.
Nor will my pleasures and joys.
This is not a lament!
It is simply the natural order of things:
that the body eventually breaks down and
inevitably dies.

To deny this, or continue living mindlessly
as if I had endless time,
or fight it, or complain, or catastrophize—
is to suffer.

But to accept this, to say "Hello" to it,
to breathe into it, and let it just be—
is to be free.

My practice since then has been to recite this twice each day. Prior to this I found it extremely difficult to actually take in, on a visceral level, the fact that I will surely die. Something seems to be almost hardwired in humans that makes truly facing our death very elusive.

The illusion that we all subtly hold is that we have endless time. This leaves us convinced that our life will continue indefinitely into some vague future. We are rarely aware of the extent to which this belief keeps us skating on thin ice, oblivious to the very real fact that our lives can end or be drastically altered at any time, without any warning or preparation.

It keeps us in the state of "waking sleep," cruising through life in a numbing automatic way, so that we don't have to experience the anxiety of facing the certainty that we will die.

THIS ANXIETY IS CERTAINLY UNDERSTANDABLE. Our survival instinct is to continue to live, and while this instinct can help us when danger arises, it also stands in direct conflict with the fact of our mortality. This conflict tends to bring discomfort, and since our desire to avoid discomfort is very strong, we mostly put the fact of our death out of our minds, perhaps doing everything we can to avoid it through the endless pursuit of pleasure, diversion, and busyness.

Even when we get a visceral inkling that we don't have forever, within a nanosecond the insight is replaced with thoughts about something we have to do, or the trip we have planned, or even something as mundane as what we want for dinner. All of this serves to affirm our aliveness, and keep awareness of death and impermanence out of consciousness.

On an intellectual level, we know we're going to die—yet we don't really know it on a visceral or experiential level. So the truth of our inevitable death is rarely taken in, again, because we fear that it might lead to overwhelming anxiety.

To help us avoid this anxiety, and to help us remain oblivious, we humans often adopt the unique and peculiar delusion that we are "special"—in the sense that death and the particular challenges that can precede death don't apply to us.

We would, of course, probably deny that we believe this. Yet, even while we might readily admit that we are all subject to the biological process that birth inevitably ends in death, on a day-to- day level, we nonetheless remain oblivious to our mortality.

I WAS a hospice volunteer for ten years, and in my many encounters with the patients who were expected to die within a short time, I only met one person who wasn't caught in some form of denial. Even though death was on the immediate horizon, most seemed to need to hold on to the unconscious belief that they still had plenty of time.

The fact that we can maintain this stance even when death is looming is evidence of our mind's brilliant talent for avoidance. As T. S. Eliot said: "Humankind cannot bear very much reality."

CERTAIN CLASSIC BELIEF systems have evolved in most cultures to shield us from the anxiety, and sometimes even the panic, of actually confronting the fact that we will die. Whether we believe that we go to heaven, rejoin with God, or become part of some vast cosmic energy, the purpose of these belief systems is to give us the comfort that through our spiritual perpetuation we don't really die, and thus we can avoid confronting death as the end of "me."

Religious belief systems are certainly not the only way we make ourselves feel somehow "special"—in the sense of being invulnerable. Some identify strongly with their race or country. This allows us to feel that we're part of something that will continue into the indefinite future.

Others may find a similar comfort from identifying with a higher cause or even with a leader. Some find this comfort in having children who will carry on their legacy, or in the thought that they will live on in the hearts of those they have loved or helped, or in writing books or making art—anything that gives a sense of immortality to "me."

Although these various comforts may give us a temporary respite, we can't deny that they can also be a subtle way of trying to avoid facing the facts, and our fears, around dying.

Denial isn't the only motive for these things; however, to the extent that it is, we need to acknowledge it to live more honestly and authentically in our remaining years.

DESPITE THE STRONG instinctual aversion to facing our own death, as well as the deeply embedded cultural protections, most of the wisdom traditions agree that we ultimately have to come to grips with the visceral understanding that we will, in fact, die.

Many even emphasize the view that this understanding can be truly transformative. But for this to happen, we may have to experience some kind of life crisis—something to push us out of our complacency and challenge our illusions.

It may take the death of someone close to us, or a serious illness, to bring us closer to an inner understanding that we will with certainty one day die, and that we can't avoid the fact that we are not special in this regard. When we are jolted out of our complacency by a life-altering crisis, we may feel lost and betrayed, and at the time, it may be hard to see how this experience could possibly make our life better.

. . .

I HAD an experience like this right after I had surgery for kidney cancer. Because of the complications and comorbidities from the surgery, I had chronic and sometimes intense nerve pain that persisted for several years. It was out of this experience that I realized the need to honestly examine my relationship to death.

I was fortunate, because I still had the time and energy needed to process all the resistance and detours that arise when we begin to face our mortality. If we wait until we have a terminal diagnosis, it may be too late to begin the work of trying to live more authentically.

We don't have to make this mistake. At some point, living a life of complacency, busyness, and diversions may no longer be satisfying, and we may naturally begin to revisit our priorities. This can sometimes be painful—yet recognizing this may also give us the freedom to choose to live in a new way.

REGARDLESS OF OUR age or state of health, making the effort to acknowledge our inevitable death is a good beginning. Just as a life crisis can add poignancy to our day-to-day experience, so does the change in perspective that comes with recognizing our mortality.

What this will look like is very individual; for some it may mean making the effort to communicate more genuinely with those we care about the most. It could mean devoting more time to prayer or meditation, or whatever brings us closer to living in the present, with a greater appreciation for life.

The realization that we don't want to put off living in accord with what is most important to us can help us be grateful for what we value most, rather than continuing to indulge the fears that keep us from living most genuinely.

WHEN THE REALITY of our aging can no longer be denied and we experience the disappointment of failing bodies and declining minds, our natural inclination is to complain, catastrophize, or wallow in self-pity. But does it ever help to complain or indulge in self- pity? Doesn't it guarantee that we will suffer?

The same is true as we try to fight each new piece of evidence that we are not immune to aging—trying to cover the wrinkles and sags and bulges or searching for exotic remedies for realities that are just part of how life unfolds. Even exercising can be a form of fighting against the inevitable.

I'm not saying we shouldn't exercise or do whatever we can to keep the body healthy; it's only problematic when we have the mindset that our efforts will stop the inevitable decline.

Some people push themselves hard in an attempt to overcome whatever symptoms they may have. When we think of ourselves as strong, we may believe that we can override our perceived weaknesses. But this is just foolish, since it comes out of pride and the fear of being—or appearing—weak. At some point it has to become obvious that we can't remain healthy or youthful forever. Trying to get our old life back just leads to unhappiness, and the unhappiness continues and deepens as we try to fight the inevitable again and again.

Isn't it true that we always suffer when we fight against things that we cannot change?

. . .

When we see our life and death as a natural process—that life is finite and that dying is to be expected—it becomes easier to take in, and to see more and more in clear perspective. That is the first step in acceptance. It starts as conceptual knowledge and then, as it becomes more and more embodied, it deepens into an understanding grounded in the body and in the heart.

This is a gradual process, which is why I recite the reflection two times each and every day. In this sense it is like a prayer, but the only thing I'm asking for is true understanding.

Nietzsche and Heidegger wrote extensively on the need to embrace death head-on in order to truly experience what life really is. They affirm the view that without a real awareness of our death, we are not really alive.

Normally we identify with and indulge our fear-based thoughts and emotions, but as we embrace death's unavoidability, these thoughts and emotions, which normally seem so real and so solid, become more and more porous and insubstantial.

Although the unfolding confrontation with the reality of death may sound grim, in actual fact, it is grimmer to sleepwalk through life, missing out on the richness and depth of living from kindness, appreciation, and love—the qualities that emerge more readily when we live with honesty.

By facing death squarely, we paradoxically free ourselves of the anxiety that surrounds death and begin to learn to live more authentically. Even if our transcendence is not complete or permanent, we may still enjoy a degree of freedom from anxiety that we have never thought possible.

. . .

EVEN THOUGH I'VE had many friends and relatives die in the last twenty years, and witnessed dozens of deaths as a hospice volunteer, these experiences did not have the same effect on me as doing the "Reflection on Death." More than anything, doing the "Reflection" has helped dispel the deeply embedded illusion that I have endless time.

For me, reflecting on my death every day has been a process of turning away from complacency and turning toward what is most important. In this process I've been forced to look at myself with a penetrating honesty, which includes facing the fears that have held me back from living from my true heart.

In reflecting on how I want to spend my remaining time and energy, what I've discovered is that reminding myself every day that we are surely going to die can ultimately direct me toward clarity and love.

As a result of doing the "Reflection" there are definite changes in my priorities and life perspective, as well as subtle changes in how I am now living my life. There is more honesty in my relationships, less dwelling on petty worries, and less willingness to allow anger or fear to dictate my life. I definitely feel lighter, with more equanimity, am more appreciative, and am certainly less entitled. Probably most important, I am able to increasingly experience and express love more readily.

In this sense, "Reflection on Death" is not so much about dying as it is about learning how to live fully.

THROUGHOUT THE "REFLECTION ON DEATH" there is no mention of what death is or what might come after we die. The truth is: I don't know. In fact, I don't know if anybody really knows. But this shouldn't stop us from doing the essential work of looking at our own relationship to the fact that we will someday surely die.

Reflecting on our death is another way of asking, "Do I want to stay stuck in complacency and fear, or do I want to follow the path of living from a more open heart?"

41

THREE LIFE-AFFIRMING EXERCISES

The following exercises relating to your death might prove to be not only interesting but potentially transformative.

Your Timeline

Draw a horizontal line on a page representing the time from birth to death. Write the word *Birth* on the far left of the line and *Death* on the far right. Place a short vertical line where you imagine you are on this timeline.

First, reflect on what this means for a few moments—to feel the reality that you don't have endless time.

Next, given the amount of time you imagine you have left, write down any reprioritizing that you may think is called for. When you're finished, reflect on what you want to do differently going forward.

. . .

Your Obituary

Write a short obituary—just five to six sentences—on your qualities as a person, as if they were written by someone who really knew you. Write it as if you died today. When finished, consider if it provides any insight into yourself that might make a difference in how you live.

Your Tombstone

Write down what you would ideally like to have written about you on your tombstone, even if you don't plan to have one—just one short sentence.

This one line represents your highest aspiration, and it is something that is worthwhile to consider every day.

42

APPRECIATION

Once, when I was in the throes of a relapse of my immune system disorder, I had the good fortune to remember that my pain was no different from the pain we all share.

At that point the depth of my misunderstanding became very clear: I may not like my experience and I can try to push it away, but the fact remains that whatever is happening right now, regardless of how unpleasant it is, is my genuine life.

Whether or not the small mind wants it is not the point; to live most authentically requires that we honestly embrace our life, exactly as it is.

Part of appreciating those we are closest to has to include the awareness that our time together is limited. We have no idea what will happen, or when, which is again the theme of skating on thin ice.

But this fact doesn't have to make us morose. In fact, knowing that our time is limited allows us to appreciate one another all the more. I remember a few years ago when Elizabeth and I were on a wonderful retreat-vacation in the beautiful area of Lake Como, in northern Italy. We spent hours walking through idyllic little towns, eating pasta at almost every meal, meditating in a different church each day, and appreciating how lucky we were to have the health and resources to share our life together. Then, shortly after our return to San Diego, Elizabeth was diagnosed with breast cancer.

EVEN THOUGH ELIZABETH responded to this with very little melodrama, I nonetheless remember feeling as if the ground had been pulled out from under me. And in spite of my many years of practicing with my own illness, I couldn't deny that I was still somewhat caught up in the illusion that we had endless time.

This illusion, which we all have to some degree, leaves us convinced that our life will continue indefinitely into the vague future. We are rarely aware of the extent to which this belief keeps us skating on thin ice, oblivious of the very real fact that our lives can end or be drastically altered at any time, without any warning.

As we become increasingly aware that we and our loved ones have limited time, we are bound to have times of feeling groundless and disconnected. I certainly felt the fear of disconnection and loss when I was told Elizabeth had cancer.

BUT WE CAN'T FORGET that true connection comes when we're willing to acknowledge these uncomfortable feelings that are part of our human condition. True connection comes when we breathe the aching fear of loss into the center of our chests and simply let it be there, no matter how uncomfortable we might feel.

Once we truly learn to reside in our fear of aloneness, we will no longer expect those close to us to take away our fears. Instead, we will know real intimacy, which can never be based on neediness or the fear of being alone. When we relate to people from the small mind of neediness, we can't truly love them or appreciate them.

True appreciation requires the courage to face our discomforts and our fears. It is what ultimately allows us to live most authentically.

OVER THE COURSE of traveling the path of self-realization, we may forget this many times and find ourselves going off course. But we can't judge ourselves for each wayward detour.

Each detour, each backslide, is actually part of the path of learning and growth. If we are to affirm our life, to say Yes to it, we must say Yes to *all* of it. Each detour and backslide is an integral part of the whole; would we be who we are today if we hadn't learned from our so-called mistakes and flaws?

Living authentically means we're acknowledging the whole of what our life is, and being willing to truly live it, just as it is. The key, of course, is to cease resistance to what is.

When I finally understood this in relation to my illness and to Elizabeth's cancer, I became willing to affirm that I was on board for the trip. Whether I liked the trip or not, I could still appreciate the ride—to see what it was like and where it was going, without the extra baggage of self-pity and fear.

Self-pity, the complaints and judgments, and especially all of the fears, are the real obstacles to surrendering to what is. They are also what prevent genuine appreciation for our life.

I LEARNED MUCH about appreciation from my time with Mary, who was a sixty-nine-year-old hospice patient with heart disease and emphysema. On one visit, while we were watching a video, I felt the impulse to hold her hand. Then I hesitated, thinking it might make her feel uncomfortable. When I got home later, I felt sorry that I had held myself back. Resolving not to let my doubts and anxieties get in the way the next time, I began to look forward to holding her hand and to having a warm visit. But the day I was to go see her again, I received a call that Mary had just died.

What affected me more than the sadness I felt at her death was the realization that I would never again have the opportunity to make the simple gesture of touching her hand. I had given in to the doubts of my small mind, and by the time I had become aware of this, it was too late to express my open heart.

THE LESSON WAS clear and powerful: time swiftly passes by, and with it, our only chance. The words that were painfully etched into my being, and that subsequent hospice visits brought up time and time again, were "Don't hold back your heart in fear."

There is a message that all of us need to hear over and over again: "Time is fleeting. Don't hold back. Appreciate this precious life." The wish of every teacher is for all of us to be able to take these words to heart.

This is the kind of appreciation that artist Paul Klee

described when he said, "Imagine that you are dead. After many years of exile, you are permitted to cast a single glance earthward. You see a lamppost and an old dog lifting his leg against it. You are so moved that you cannot stop sobbing."

In an imperfect world there are rare moments like these when we understand that All Is One, and perhaps that All Is Love. In the stillness of those moments, where life shimmers in its clarity, we know that, paradoxically, life is perfect just as it is, even in its imperfection.

These moments do not require anything more than ceasing the internal dialogue that keeps us caught in the past or the future. We just need to pause, be present, and open to what is always right in front of us.

43

REFLECTIONS ON GETTING OLDER

I'm now in my late seventies, and though I often don't feel that old, I can't deny that there are many difficulties associated with getting older. Perhaps we can start by asking, what makes getting older so potentially difficult?

Certainly, as part of the menu of aging, there will be loss and the grief that follows it—grief not just for the loss of loved ones, but also for the loss of our youth, our health, our appearance, and our feelings of significance.

For some there will be loneliness and helplessness. Often, there may be anxiety and depression, especially around the uncertainty of what the future will bring. Many feel the world is changing so fast, especially technologically, that they feel left behind.

For all, there will probably be some degree of pain and an increasing sense of the finality of death.

. . .

BUT WITH ADVANCES in the medical field, being older no longer means that we are necessarily sick and incapacitated—or that we have to withdraw from active pursuits.

For some, old age may be a new stage of life—*a stage of renewal*—in which our inner life can be experienced as being of equal importance with our outer life. This gives us the possibility of understanding what this life is really about, including our place within it.

There's the possibility that we can understand, on the deepest level, that the gradual breaking down of the body is to be expected as part of the natural order of things.

And then, when it happens, instead of fighting it, there's the possibility of learning to accept it with equanimity, realizing that our new difficulties don't mean that our life is now over.

I've begun to think of older age as life in a kind of natural monastery, where I can devote this time to a deeper inner quest—the essence of monastery life.

I now prioritize having fewer distractions, leaving more time for meditation, prayer, reading, and writing, as well as being in nature. Consequently, I can now look at my life in terms of the positive qualities of getting older.

THERE IS ANOTHER USEFUL TEACHING, often attributed to the Buddha, that we can use as a guiding principle in our older years:

"In the end this is what matters most: How well did you love?"

With this in mind, as we learn to cultivate a new way of seeing, we learn to always aim toward love. The question is: How do we do this?

. . .

Perhaps we think there is some secret formula or that we have to do something special to bring love to the fore, but the only "secret" is in learning how to see and relate to whatever our life is right now in a new way. Instead of seeing our setbacks as defeats, we learn to say Yes to them —meaning we're willing to accept them and work with them.

This has to include even the things we find difficult, the things we don't want—including the mind that seems to be slipping.

When we can work with our own self-defeating attitudes around our difficulties, love is more likely to be available to us.

In this way, disappointment can often become our greatest teacher. The crisis of facing the changes that come as we get older can be reframed; from a fresh perspective they can be seen as an opportunity for inner growth and renewal.

We learn to view discomfort as a pathway to learn and open. We can come to understand that disappointment and pain can actually be tenderizers for the heart, awakening us to love.

Even the loss of our physical strength and stamina, which we at first lament, can be seen differently. When we can no longer always be on the go and have to take more and more periods of rest, instead of seeing this as a sign of our decline, we have the opportunity to see it as part of the natural process—a process that now provides us with a time for increased reflection and inward awareness.

This is a radical change in how we relate to our experience. Now, for me, when I'm tired, I no longer experience it as "the beginning of the end." It has become easier to welcome and embrace the time as a chance to slow down and be truly present.

I've learned that living genuinely doesn't require that I *do* something; all it requires is that I learn how to just *be*.

This is one of the great benefits of aging—being able to experience the deep satisfaction of occupying a space without an agenda; being able to enjoy the inner equanimity of just Being, regardless of how or where we find ourselves.

When Elizabeth and I visited the remains of the concentration camp at Auschwitz, it was a very sobering experience. Before we left, I picked up a handful of small stones from the mostly barren grounds and brought them home with me. I started the practice of carrying one of the stones in my pocket, and when I would find myself caught in emotional distress, I would put my hand in my pocket and feel the stone—reminding myself of the universality of human suffering.

At one point, I put one of the stones on the table right beside me where I have consultations with students, and sometimes when a student would describe their difficulties, after talking to them for a while, I would give them the stone—telling them how I use mine. My hope was that it would serve as a reminder of the suffering we all share, and perhaps somewhat ease the experience of distress they were feeling.

We don't have to have a stone from a concentration camp as a reminder; we could use any artifact that has some personal meaning for us. The point is to be able to bring a somewhat larger perspective to what we're feeling.

Some losses may feel as if they knock us to the ground. For example, it is natural as we get older for our sexual desires to gradually diminish. For many, especially men, this can feel as if our life is over, like our last vestige of youth is now gone.

With the loss of our youthful appearance—where we have to accept that we are getting grayer or more wrinkled—we have the opportunity to work on our attachment to the need to appear appealing. As we breathe this sense of loss into the heart center, we may come to the very freeing realization that the need to appear appealing simply doesn't matter. What a relief!

The same may be true with our deep attachment to feeling youthful. Certainly, having more energy and stamina feels better than being tired, but as we work with what we sometimes think of painfully as our "lost youth," we may begin to appreciate our newfound ability to slow down and simply be—something that is rarely possible when we have the energy to stay constantly on the go.

We all dread the helplessness of losing control; yet, real freedom lies in recognizing the futility of demanding that life be within our control.

Instead, we must learn the willingness to feel—and to say Yes to—the experience of helplessness itself. This is one of the hidden gifts of serious illness or loss. It pushes us right to our edge, where we may have the good fortune to realize that our only real option is to surrender to our experience and let it just be.

. . .

One year Elizabeth and I took a trip to Barcelona. At the time, I had an intestinal infection, including a fairly intense bout of diarrhea, but we decided to go anyway. Once we got to Barcelona, the diarrhea got worse, and even though I really should have stayed in the apartment we had rented, instead we took a train to visit a monastery. Halfway there, I knew I had to get off the train to use the toilet, but when we entered the train station, it was mostly deserted and the bathrooms were locked. To my great humiliation, I pooped in my pants—a literal example of the popular expression, "Shit happens."

We had to walk several blocks to find a restaurant with a bathroom. To add to my humiliation the bathroom was out of toilet paper, but Elizabeth wasn't the least bit perturbed, and she proceeded to clean me up with the many tissues in her bag.

I had thought I could never go through something like that, but being helpless can be a great teacher. My only choice was to have the experience be exactly as it was, and to realize that my pride had to be surrendered. Once I was no longer identified with being strong and independent, instead of feeling horrible, we both were able to take the situation much more lightly, and the experience transformed from one of helplessness and powerlessness to one of genuine intimacy.

Another example: For years after I had surgery for kidney cancer, I had to deal with PTSD from the pain I experienced during some highly invasive procedures while I was in the hospital. For a long time, I had to close my eyes when scenes from hospitals came on the TV. I just wanted to disappear when images of the painful procedures would pop back into my mind.

As anyone with PTSD knows, the helplessness can easily turn into paralysis. In my case the helplessness was exacerbated by having to deal with the comorbidities, the medications, and the side effects of the medications—not knowing what to expect, not being able to plan beyond a few hours. It often left me with a vague sense of doom whenever I thought about the future.

The loss of my physical strength intensified the feeling of powerlessness, and along with the doom I also experienced the world as a dangerous place—who knew what was coming next? This is a common experience for those dealing with similar circumstances where strongly believed fearful thoughts increase the experience of distress.

When I would get shooting pains through the nerves in my face and head, for instance, my mind would instantly return to the automatic thoughts: "Not again!" "Will it get worse?" "Will it ever stop?" "I can't take this!"

Yet, even when things seemed really bad, I still was able—although sometimes with difficulty—to remember to breathe into the chest center and cease resisting what is. When I remembered to do this, there was always a degree of equanimity. It wasn't that the pain or the anxiety disappeared, but there was a larger sense of Being, within which I knew, on some fundamental level, that I was okay.

When we know that we are fundamentally okay, we can find value and comfort in simple, slow, and natural living. Can we see through the fog of our busyness and our vanities to reset our priorities?

. . .

THE PACIFIC OCEAN outside my door doesn't care how much money I have. The nearby mountains couldn't care less about my appearance. The California poppies keep growing regardless of my social status. The sky is not the least concerned about my imperfections. With this in mind, why can't we accept ourselves just as we are?

Acceptance is about surrendering to the truth of what is happening right now. It gives us perspective—to see things for how big or small they really are, whether they really matter, and whether to nourish them or no longer hold onto them.

BENEATH ALL OF our resistance to change is fear of failure and fear of losing control. Yet, trying to hold on to the past or present is pointless since change is inevitable. Why waste energy worrying about what you don't have or about things that don't really matter? That is the root to unhappiness.

Instead, we could pay attention to the good already present in our life, and do our best at whatever we are doing. There is satisfaction and joy in that.

There can even be satisfaction in aging. It's okay to get old. We're supposed to get old—it's the natural order of things.

It's okay to know we are not going to be here forever because that helps us treasure the time we do have, and find virtue or meaning in our lives.

Finding beauty in everyday life is key; we do this by simply slowing down and looking at all of the things we can appreciate. We may find the great value of simple, slow, and natural living.

. . .

RETURNING to the words of the Buddha: he exhorted us to remember that we are not here forever, and that we should remind ourselves that each day could be our last.

The truth is, we have no idea how long we have. We never know what will happen next. We don't even know what's right around the corner.

But if we remember that we have limited time, we can begin to understand that each day is precious, and that we should never take anyone or anything for granted.

We can stop wasting so much of our life replaying the past, worrying about the future, or staying stuck in complacency. As a longtime hospice volunteer, I can't even the count the number of times I witnessed patients dying with regret.

For all of us, in all of our relationships, why would we want to continue our self-centered and small-minded behaviors toward others when any one of us could die at any time? All we need to do is look into another's eyes and remember:

Everyone has pain. Everyone suffers. Everyone will die.

Love is what remains when we can experience another as they truly are, without judgment.

WHEN WE ARE able to cultivate the experience of connectedness, we can tap into one aspect of what is considered the deepest wisdom: that "All is One."

As we take this understanding into the heart, particularly as we can feel into the suffering that all of us share, we can tap into the other aspect of deepest wisdom: that "All is Love."

Again, returning to the words often purported to be from the Buddha: "In the end this is what matters most: How well did you love?"

. . .

It is essential to remember that we're all beginners when it comes to aging, and like all beginners, we often will have to start again at square one. Yet there can be comfort in understanding the wisdom that there are no Big Answers that are going to explain the mystery of life or take away our pain or our dark nights.

For me, it's enough to know that this sometimes wonderful, sometimes difficult journey is really not so complicated. We are born, we live, and then we die—this is the natural order of things. And everything in between —including all of our struggles and difficulties—is also part of the natural order of things.

Again, everyone has pain. Everyone suffers. And everyone will die. When we don't understand this, we take all of the in-between things much too seriously.

My wish for everyone is this: to truly take seriously just one thing, which is the commitment to living, as best we can, from kindness and love.

44

SOYEZ ZEN—DROPPING THE PRISON WALLS

Several years ago, I heard a story about an older man who in his early teens had lived in a home for juvenile offenders in Northern California. What he remembered most about this home was visiting day. Every Sunday, friends and relatives could come visit the boys. Every Sunday, he would look out through a large knothole in the wooden fence to see who was coming. But nobody ever came to visit him.

Reflecting back on this time of his life, all he could remember was the sadness, desolation, and loneliness that he had felt when he was looking through that knothole.

As this young boy grew up, he led a very hard life. He entered into a life of crime and was in and out of jail. But in his middle years, he began to learn from his difficulties and somehow turned his direction completely around. In his later years, he went back to the home in Northern California to revisit the experiences of his youth.

This time when he went into the yard and looked

through the hole in the fence, what he saw was the hillside with its rolling green grass and majestic old oak trees. Essentially, he saw the beauty of the world.

This story is a good reminder that when we're caught in our self-centered dream—wanting, needing, obsessing on our "self"—we're seeing things as *we* are, not as *they* are.

We see them through our own hole in the fence, our filtered perceptions clouded by believed thoughts and emotional reactions. But as we follow the path of self-discovery, we begin to see reality more and more clearly. We begin to see things more as they really are, and with that clarity, a deepened appreciation frequently arises.

LET'S come at this from a different perspective. I once heard that on a clear night we can see, at best, about two thousand stars. But modern astronomy has discovered that in our galaxy alone there are 400 billion stars! That's a big number to imagine. The real kicker is that our galaxy, with its 400 billion stars, is only one of 400 billion galaxies.

I may be off by a few billion, but it's a pretty big picture nevertheless. What comes to mind are the words of Humphrey Bogart at the end of *Casablanca.* He said something like: "It doesn't take much to see that our problems don't amount to a hill of beans in this crazy world."

It's essential that we bring the big picture to mind once in a while, if only to remind us of what we tend to forget. Unity consciousness, our basic connectedness, enlightenment—whatever we want to call it—isn't some "thing" that we either have or don't. It's not necessary to connect with the 400 billion galaxies to step beyond our own boundary.

We can realize our capacity for enlarged awareness in small doses—by experiencing the song of a bird, feeling a cool breeze on a warm day, looking into the eyes of a newborn baby, sharing the pain of another being. Every event of our daily life is an opportunity to connect with the vastness of Being.

HUMPHREY BOGART'S character was making an important point. When we forget how small our drama is, we're likely to lose ourselves in a narrow view of spiritual practice—trying to change, trying to get, trying to do. Living on this level often becomes all too serious.

The point is not to ignore our difficulties—disappointment is still the best teacher. But we don't have to get lost in our suffering. Working with it isn't the only way to wake up; life is too short to close the door on other possibilities. If we think we can't really open the door until we work with everything that gets in the way, we forget that we'll always be clearing the path, until we die.

Tasting the essence of each moment teaches us that yes, we *are* this body, with all of our difficulties; but at the same time, we are much, much more. And the essence of the moment is as available from changing a hose in the garden or walking down a busy street in the middle of the city as it is from gazing at the stars or sitting in meditation for a week.

IN A WAY, we get good at what we practice, and what we've been practicing our whole lives is making a big drama out of a little hill of beans. Now we have the opportunity to practice something else: working with that drama when necessary, to be sure, but not just getting lost in that aspect of practice.

Instead, we can cultivate a curiosity for the unknown, stay open to tasting the Vastness, and not lose sight of the bigger picture. What is the bigger picture? It's looking through the knothole of a fence without the filter of our conditioned judgments, being able to see what's there—the wonder of the world.

ONCE WHEN ELIZABETH and I were in Paris, we saw a large billboard in the subway station that read *Soyez Zen*. Literally this means "Be Zen." It could be interpreted more generally as "Just Live," or "Appreciate the Sweetness of the Moment."

Although the billboard was just an advertisement for futons, it made me realize how often we forget that spiritual practice is actually about *living*, about opening into *whatever* life presents. Instead, we tend to equate spiritual practice with either a particular technique, such as sitting in meditation, or with feeling a particular way, such as calm or centered.

HAVE you heard about the little bird sitting on your shoulder who asks, "Is today the day you're going to die?"

This is not a somber bird, nor is it asking the question in a dramatic way. Ever so lightly, it's telling us that living the genuine life is about *living*.

This bird is giving us a message we need to hear over and over again: Time is fleeting. Don't hold back. Appreciate this precious life.

We are truly living when we can experience the vividness of life—the quiet texture of simply being.

Only by residing in what is, exactly as it is, will our self-imposed prison walls come down. And when they do, all that remains is the connectedness that we are.

EPILOGUE

THE ESSENTIAL REMINDERS

Each of these aphorisms represents a key point to be assimilated on the path of self-realization. Taken together, they serve as a summary of the main practices described in this book. One very helpful way to use these reminders is to pick one each day, returning to the phrase over and over again during the day to remind yourself of what is most important.

- Remember your aspiration; without it there will only be sleep.
- Perseverance is the key, not how you feel.
- Don't try to change; just be aware.
- The fundamental question: Can I reside in my experience right now?
- Say Yes to difficulties; they are not obstacles on the path; they *are* the path.
- Drop the story line of "me."
- Cultivate mercy toward yourself; compassion toward others will follow.

- Be present as often as possible; stay there as long as possible.
- The cardinal rule in relationships: refrain from blaming.
- Until you become intimate with your fears, they will always limit your ability to love.
- Reside in the Heart—not thinking, not doing—just Being.
- When you really pay attention, *everything* is your teacher.
- In this very moment, what would it mean to live from kindness?

ACKNOWLEDGMENTS

I'd like extend to my most heartfelt thanks to Cornelia Feye, my editor and publisher at Konstellation Press. She has done a terrific job of guiding me through the new terrain of Indie publishing.

And as always, I'm truly grateful to Elizabeth Hamilton, my wife and spiritual partner, who has not only been a very able editor, but who has also encouraged me throughout the process of writing this book.

ABOUT THE AUTHOR

Ezra Bayda was born in Atlantic City, N.J., and graduated from Rutgers University with a degree in philosophy. At 26 he became a carpenter, and later a general contractor, a profession he stayed in for thirty years. He began meditating in 1970, and lived in a Gurdjieff community for several years, after which he became a full time Zen student. He began teaching and writing in 1995, and for eighteen years, along with his wife and co-teacher Elizabeth Hamilton, ran the Zen Center San Diego. During this time, he wrote seven critically acclaimed award-winning books, including *Being Zen* and *Aging for Beginners.* He was also a Hospice volunteer for ten years. He and Elizabeth now live in a retirement community in La Jolla, Ca., and teach meditation by zoom. He also enjoys daily walks along the ocean, cooking and playing ping pong.

ALSO BY EZRA BAYDA

Being Zen, Shambhala Publications

At Home in the Muddy Water, Shambhala

Saying Yes to Life, Wisdom Publications

Zen Heart, Shambhala Publicagtions

Beyond Happiness, Shambhala Publications

The Authentic Life, Shambhala Publications

Aging for Beginners, Wisdom Publications

Selected material from the above books is included in Skating on Thin Ice

www.ingramcontent.com/pod-product-compliance
Lightning Source LLC
LaVergne TN
LVHW091719070526
838199LV00050B/2456

* 9 7 9 8 9 8 6 8 4 3 2 1 6 *